From Salford to Tucson

and back again

The globetrotting memoirs of a Manchester United fanatic

Robert Carter

Copyright © 2009 Robert Carter. All rights reserved. No part of this book may be reproduced or retransmitted in any form or by any means without the written consent of the publisher.

International Standard Book Number ISBN 978-0-557-04259-3

CONTENTS

Introduction

A Quick History Lesson

The Early Sixties

The Trinity

Learning To Play

The World Cup Final and World Cup Willie

The 67 Title and New Hope

Champions of Europe

A Ten Year Old Standing On The Stretford End

When Love Is Not Enough – Poor Old Wilf

Farewell Bobby

The Worst Year of Our Lives

The Doc's New Team and New Hope

Cookes, Swinton Town and Old Traffordians

When Love is Too Much

Dave Sexton

Gold, Champagne and Big Ron

There's Only One Bryan Robson

Big Norm and Kevin for PM

Sports Report and Why You Should Never Leave Early

When The Skinflints Cost Us The League

The Second Dynasty

Michael Knighton, Robert Maxwell and Rupert Murdock

Moving To Cambridge and a New Kind of Banter

Super Lee Martin

Rotterdam

Another Reason To Hate Leeds

Twenty Six Bloody Years

The First Double, Living In DC, and Meeting a Future Legend

Another Double and The Arndale

Hail Le Roi

Living and Playing in The Desert

American Sports

Travelling the World

Thank God for Satellite and T'Internet

Scaring the Neighbours

The Treble and Almost Kicking The Bucket

The Commonwealth Games

Los Angeles

Ronnie's Debut

Ye Olde Jolly Carter's and Millwall

Return of The Prodigal

Champions of Europe – Again

The Future is Bright

Introduction

As we get older, the most important thing we have is our memories. This is a book about my memories, particularly those around Manchester United Football Club. If you are a United fan, you will no doubt relate to many of the stories, and you will enjoy reading about them from the personal viewpoint of a fellow supporter. As a United fan you will enjoy re-living the emotional rollercoaster that our beloved football club puts us through. If for some strange reason you don't follow football, this will give you an insight into the psyche of the football supporter. If you support somebody other than United, why?

There are many reasons why we support a football team and we often can't put those reasons into words. Sometimes as a youngster we have a favorite player and support the team they play for. Sometimes it happens in the school playground where we like the colour of a shirt (although this reason totally baffles me). Other times it is because we, as Brits, like to support the underdog.

For me though it is easy. I was born in Davyhulme, grew up in Swinton, now part of Salford, and went to a school where 90% of the boys were United fans. I know this will dispel the popular myth that people in Manchester don't support United but who cares. As Mancunians we know the truth.

Whatever the reason that you support your team; there is no doubt that the history of Manchester United is one without rival. We have suffered more tragedy than any other club and thankfully, we have had more triumph than most. Our history is one of the main reasons why we are supported by millions throughout the world. The other reason, no matter what the circumstance, Manchester United will always play the game the right way. From Busby's magnificent Babes through to the current team, United have been unrivalled in their passion for open, attractive and entertaining football.

For fan or foe, the Manchester United story is one of highs and lows, of excitement, adventure and legends. This version of the story is one through the eyes of an ordinary fan like you. It is not the autobiography of a player yet to reach his prime, or one that will never be anywhere near as good as his ego lets him believe. It is not written by a journalist, or anybody with an insider view. All the stories are true, some joyous and some painful. Like every other United fan that I know, I live and breathe football. I cry when we win and I cry even louder when we lose.

So here is my story as I follow our glorious football team that is Manchester United, Enjoy!

A Quick History Lesson

I was born in January 1960, less than two years after the disaster at Munich. The legends who lost their lives that day should have been the first team I supported. I should have watched Tommy Taylor and Duncan Edwards in their prime, but like millions of others, I was robbed of that privilege. This is however, not a story of maybes and what if's, it is a true story about my love affair with Manchester United. My story obviously begins in the early sixties, when I started to play, watch and love football, but before I can tell it, I need to share a few facts and a little history.

Manchester United is the biggest football club in the world. In fact, they are by far the biggest sports franchise in the world. This has major advantages, like the ability to sell merchandise all over the world, but it also has disadvantages like losing its identity as a local team. I personally will take the wealth, as long as it continues to be invested in the team, but there is an air of sadness when half the accents at Old Trafford don't speak properly.

United have been champions of Europe three times and have won the Premiership ten times, more than anybody else by a country mile. They have also won more FA Cups than any other team and are the only English team to be crowned Champions of the world, and they have achieved this glory twice. United have the biggest club stadium in Britain, holding more than 76,000 and this is way too small for most games. I've been disappointed so many times when I've failed to get a ticket to a big game. Applications are usually over-subscribed and the ballot seems to skip my membership number with glaring regularity. Old Trafford would easily fill 100,000 if there was a sensible way of expanding the stadium.

The current team is made up of millionaire superstars but this has not always been the case. In fact, they have not always been called Manchester United. Surprisingly, they have not always played in the famous red shirts either; their first kit was green and gold, reflecting the colours of the industrial company where it all began in a suburb of Manchester. In the nineteenth century, Manchester was the heartbeat of England. The industrial revolution was born in Manchester and it was the most productive industrial city in the world. Manchester was also the birthplace of the railway.

In 1878, a group of football mad railway workers created their own football club. They were called, Newton Heath L.Y.R. (Lancashire and Yorkshire Railway). Newton Heath was denied entry into the Football League on several occasions and because of the lack of ability to take on the wealthy teams of the day, they struggled financially. Like so many twists and turns in the United legend, this adversity led to opportunity and the birth of success. Club Captain Henry Stafford took his St Bernard dog to a fund raising event for the ailing club. The event itself barely broke even, and worst still, the dog went missing. A few days later the dog was discovered at the home of local brewer and wealthy businessman, Henry Davies. When Davies, a rugby and bowls fan, met with Henry Stafford, he was intrigued by the clubs story and bought them, injecting much needed cash. Like many a traveler on his last legs, Newton Heath had been saved by a St Bernard dog.

Henry Davies also moved the club to a new ground at Bank Street in Clayton. This was three miles away from the railway works at Newton Heath and closer to

Manchester city centre. He decided to change the name of the club and after much soul searching the names of Manchester Central and Manchester Celtic were both turned down (thankfully) and Manchester United was born in 1902. Within two seasons United were promoted to the First Division (the premier league of its day) and in 1908, United won its first league title, now playing in the famous red shirts.

United were also moving forward off the pitch as well. In 1910, they moved from their old Bank Street Stadium to a new purpose built ground at Old Trafford. It was just in the nick of time. Two days after moving to Old Trafford, strong winds blew down the main wooden stand at Bank Street. Even in the early days, the fortunes of Manchester United would have made an Oscar winning Hollywood script.

When Old Trafford was opened on February 19th 1910 it was described as the best football stadium in the world. (It is remarkable how a century later it is still regarded as one of the best football stadiums in the world.) The cost of the 1910 version seems modest today but it was a small fortune of 60,000 pounds at the time, with a capacity of 80,000.

During the Second World War, the Luftwaffe added their bit of history to the legend by bombing the ground. It was 1949 before it re-opened; looking exactly the same as it had before the bombing. In 1950, a roof was added to the famous Stretford End which packed in 20,000 fanatical United supporters. When floodlights were installed in the late 1950's, Bobby Charlton recalled that thousands of fans were congregated outside the ground before the season had started. They just wanted to be part of the story and witness the floodlights for the first time. United has always had that type of support.

The team's fortunes were up and down throughout the 1920's and 1930's, mainly down. In 1930 they made their worst ever start to a season, losing their first twelve games, and we thought the seventies were bleak! It was in 1945 that Matt Busby joined United, having turned down Liverpool. Matt was still at the helm of the club twenty five years later.

Busby's impact was immediate, leading the team to second place in four out of five years before eventually winning the championship for the third time in the clubs history in 1952. This was the end of one era and the start of the most legendary period in the history of sport, the birth of the famous Busby Babes. The Babes redefined football, winning successive championships in 1956 and 1957.

Most of the Busby Babes had graduated through the ranks, starting with the youth team. Matt decided that although they were incredibly young, he could not leave them out of the first team. The average age of the team that won the championship in 1956 was just 22. The following year, they won it again with a teenager called Bobby Charlton now in the team. The team had eleven stars but the two stand outs were Duncan Edwards and Tommy Taylor, possibly the best two players in the world at that time. Tommy was signed from Barnsley and scored an amazing 131 goals in just 191 games. Duncan is still revered by those lucky enough to see him play as the greatest player of all time.

In 1958, United were going after their third title in a row and at the beginning of February went to Arsenal, winning 5-4 in what has since been described as the greatest game ever. Of course, it was completely overshadowed by what happened just a few days later. Having triumphantly knocked out Red Star Belgrade on their way to the European Cup semi final; disaster struck. After refueling at Munich airport, the plane crashed at just after 3 o'clock on February 6th. Twenty one people died, including seven players, David Pegg, Liam Whelan, Eddie Colman, Roger Byrne, Geoff Bent, Tommy Taylor and Mark Jones. Fifteen days later, the great Duncan Edwards joined them in heaven, dying from his wounds. The Busby Babes were cut down before they'd even reached their prime. I still cry when I watch the Pathé News report of the day. The best way I can think to describe the feelings of the nation came by way of an anonymous poem, 'The Flowers of Manchester' first published in folk magazine 'Sing' and later attributed to editor Eric Winter after his death. There is an amazing a cappella song version by Mick Groves of the Spinners folk group. Mick, a fellow Salford lad, claims his proudest ever moment was when he sang it quietly to Matt Busby and Louis Edwards (then chairman of United). Mick's song can be found easily on the internet and if you haven't heard it, make sure you have a box of tissues handy. Here are those amazing words.

'The Flowers of Manchester'

One cold and bitter Thursday in Munich, Germany,
Eight great football stalwarts conceded victory,
Eight men will never play again who met destruction there,
The flowers of English football, the flowers of Manchester

Matt Busby's boys were flying, returning from Belgrade,
This great United family, all masters of their trade,
The pilot of the aircraft, the skipper Captain Thain,

Three times they tried to take off and twice turned back again.

The third time down the runaway disaster followed close,
There was slush upon that runaway and the aircraft never rose,
It ploughed into the marshy ground, it broke, it overturned.
And eight of the team were killed as the blazing wreckage burned.

Roger Byrne and Tommy Taylor who were capped for England's side.
And Ireland's Billy Whelan and England's Geoff Bent died,
Mark Jones and Eddie Colman, and David Pegg also,
They all lost their lives as it ploughed on through the snow.

Big Duncan he went too, with an injury to his brain,
And Ireland's brave Jack Blanchflower will never play again,
The great Matt Busby lay there, the father of his team
Three long months passed by before he saw his team again.

The trainer, coach and secretary, and a member of the crew,
Also eight sporting journalists who with United flew,
and one of them Big Swifty, who we will ne'er forget,
the finest English 'keeper that ever graced the net.

Oh, England's finest football team its record truly great,
its proud successes mocked by a cruel turn of fate.
Eight men will never play again, who met destruction

there,
the flowers of English football, the flowers of Manchester.

This all happened two years before my birth in January 1960, and some fifty years later we still remember them. I have been the lead singer in many bands over the years and on several occasions tried to sing The Flowers of Manchester but I can never get through it without breaking down. God bless the Busby Babes.

The Early Sixties

They say if you can remember the sixties, you weren't there. That's a bit harsh I feel as I was only ten when the decade ended. For me the sixties were my formative years, the years when I fell in love with the worlds' greatest sport and the worlds' greatest team. My early recollections are a bit vague but I remember living in a small rented two up two down terraced house. It had a tin bath that wasn't plumbed in, and of course an outside toilet. My Dad was working as an engineer down the pit. To help make ends meet my mother worked at the local mill. When we got our first car, a Reliant three wheel van, I thought I was royalty. People laugh now but in those days, we were fortunate. Only one other family on Moorside Road in Swinton had a car.

People either walked to work, or took the bus. In those days, even the footballers had to use public transport, often arriving at Old Trafford with the fans, having a quick fag outside the ground before going inside to get ready. After the game, the players would either celebrate at The Salisbury or The Trafford, or drown their sorrows; either way, it was with the fans who had been cheering them on. That all changed with the abolition of the maximum wage. Now a footballer earns more in a week than a family of fans earn in a year, in those days, we were all equal.

For those not old enough to remember, the early sixties were bleak but optimistic. I remember walking a couple of miles to school, often through a pea soup fog where you could barely see the end of your nose. For entertainment we had the radio and the television. The television had a choice of two channels, both in black and white, and programs finished fairly early in the evening. Not that it mattered much to me as a toddler because I was usually in bed around 7pm.

United were rebuilding after the aftermath of Munich. Of the survivors, Bobby Charlton and Bill Foulkes were now regulars, and a young Nobby Stiles had made the first team. The only other football memory I have of the early sixties was the arrival of a certain blonde haired Scotsman called Dennis Law. When we beat Leicester 3-1 in the 1963 Cup Final, we really were back on the map. Dennis scored the first goal, spinning on a six pence before finding the bottom corner. As a three year old I cannot say that I watched the cup final that year, but I've seen the highlights many times and Dennis was a phenomenon, alongside a terrific centre forward called David Herd who bagged the other two.

Another distinct memory of those early days was one evening when I was listening to the radio with my mother. All of a sudden she let out a scream and yelled 'Oh My God.' President Kennedy had been assassinated, and with him went a lot of the optimism across the globe. Things like assassinations just didn't happen in those days.

In 1964 we moved out of our rented house into a much better house in Charles Street. It was a little bigger with a separate kitchen. It also had the luxury of a fully plumbed, indoor bath. It was at the end of the kitchen. The toilet of course was outdoor and it would be a few years later that we converted the upstairs to include a fully functional bathroom. We had to move because the house in Moorside Road was declared derelict and the whole row was demolished and replaced with a small block of maisonettes.

Shortly after moving into Charles Street we had the ultimate luxury, a fitted gas fire in both the living room and the front room. We also graduated to a four wheel car, a maroon Ford Anglia. This thin curly haired blonde kid with spindly legs was now the bee's knees.

The Trinity

Anybody who knows anything about football knows about the Trinity. Matt Busby in rebuilding his team had Bobby Charlton, a monster of a player with great pace and two rocket fired feet. Bobby could score a goal from anywhere and with either foot. Alongside Bobby we had Dennis Law. Dennis was an inside forward but he had so much energy that he was often seen all over the pitch. There didn't seem to be anything that Dennis couldn't do with a ball and his overhead kicks were famous the world over. Sir Alex Ferguson has regularly described Dennis as the greatest Scottish footballer ever and who am I to argue with Fergie.

In 1964 a new talent emerged. A scrawny, good looking lad from Belfast had caught the eye of Bob Bishop the famous United scout. Bishops' telegram to Matt Busby read "I think I've found you a genius." George was given a trial and signed on by United chief scout Joe Armstrong. The amazing thing is that his local club, Glentoran, rejected him for being too light and too small. Thank you Glentoran; who knows where George could have ended up if you hadn't been so blind. The legend that is George Best needs no further introduction.

George's unbelievable dribbling skills, Bobby's ability to score from anywhere, and Dennis's incredible scoring record helped the Red's to their sixth championship in 1965. It also took United back into Europe. In March 1966 they beat Benfica of Portugal 3-2 at Old Trafford. Benfica had the upper hand because they had never lost a home tie in Europe. Maybe that's because they hadn't played United and we thrashed them 5-1 in Lisbon, scoring 3 goals in the first quarter of an hour. Plaudits at the time suggested this was Georges finest ever game and it was the game that spawned the nickname 'El Beatle'. George had become the first ever football superstar, prompting Pele to describe him as the best player in the world.

This was the year that I really took an interest in the world's greatest team sport. Living just four miles from Old Trafford was incredibly exciting, and then there was the small matter of the World Cup to look forward to.

Everybody in Swinton was really looking forward to the European Cup Semi Final and we huddled round the radio to listen to our heroes' progress. Unfortunately, Partizan Belgrade hadn't read the script and after kicking us off the park and beating us 2-0 in the first leg in Yugoslavia, even the ever optimistic Matt Busby knew we had a problem. In the first leg, Dennis Law hit the woodwork but worst still, George Best limped off with an aggravation of the knee injury he'd been carrying. George was out for the rest of the season. A certain six year old was left to cry himself to sleep.

Determined to win the European Cup for United when I grew up, I remember taking my twelve panel casey (that's a leather football with laces holding it together for those of you too young to know) into the backin' the following day. This particular backin' was a narrow entryway to the back yards on Charles Street and Mulgrave Street. I kicked the ball relentlessly in the rain against the wall. Manchester is famous for drizzle but this rain was coming down like stair rods and reluctantly I had to give in when my mother called. I was playing centre forward for United in this imaginary one man game and was gutted when the game was abandoned at half time. We were beating Real Madrid a hundred and twenty six to nil and I'd scored all the goals. The beans on toast were satisfying but I knew there were more goals in me. Why do mothers always think the rain is a bad thing?

United played well in the second leg but Belgrade defended like Trojans. One of United's latest heroes, Paddy Crerand, was sent off after a fracas with a niggly Yugoslavian and although Nobby Stiles managed a late goal, it was nothing more than a consolation. United were out. If that was a bitter enough pill to swallow, we also finished the league in 4th place and made an early exit from the FA Cup. No trophies and no European Football to look forward to next season. Would Bobby Charlton be able to do anything to put things right at the World Cup?

Learning To Play

Moving to Charles Street introduced me to a new gang of lads, all a bit older than me but more than helpful in letting me join in their games of football. Initially as a goal post, then as a ball boy and eventually graduating to goalkeeper. Yatesy (Stephen Yates) lived next door and was five years older, Acker (Brian Atkins) was the same age as Yatesy and his younger brother Lionegg (Ray Atkins, given the nickname because when he was young he was as brave as a lion and as small as an egg) was three years older than me. Pete Hill, or Pie as he was known was the same age as Lionegg. All except Acker were United fans but he was a blue. They had other mates as well, all older than me, like the Topping brothers, and big Chris Powell. The only other kid about my age was Tom Allen and even he was about eighteen months older.

For a young boy it was brilliant. Our little Wembley was on Westminster Street, using the top and bottom backin's between Charles Street and Mulgrave Street as goals. During the day this was great as all the house holders on the four corners were at work; but in the evening we often got chased away. The most fearsome character lived at the bottom of our row of houses on Charles Street. He was a grave digger at Swinton Cemetery, always wore clogs that clanked as he walked, and he owned a scary black dog. The dog would often be seen a couple of yards behind our nemesis, holding a thick piece of meat between its jaws. Apparently this gross habit made the meat tender. I can't remember this fellows name but we called him Billy. If he caught us playing he would steal our ball and put a knife through it. We wished he would dig his own grave and leave us alone.

In the mid sixties, there were hardly any cars around Swinton and so our games were not interrupted that often. We would habitually play all day. Being smaller than the other lads, and obviously slower and weaker, I had to learn fast and soon became adept at controlling the ball, dribbling and passing or shooting with both feet.

A special treat was when we went to Browns field, or St Paul's cricket pitch to give it its formal name. Here, we would be joined by other kids, including my friend from school Andrew Smith, or Smicker as we called him. Smicker and I were always the last two to be picked in any game, but we didn't care, we were playing football with the big kids, occasionally we would even score a goal. Later, Smicker would play left half and I would play right half for the all conquering Mossfield Junior School, but more of that later.

Learning to play with older kids was great for me; it meant I learned to do the basics well and not to be scared of tackling anybody, no matter how big they were. Unfortunately, it also meant that I occasionally got hurt including one time when Acker missed the ball in a wild swing and caught me on the shin. Forty plus years later I still have a lump on the shin bone.

The World Cup Final and World Cup Willie

After the disappointment of the domestic season in 1966, we all looked forward to the World Cup. Watching England play brought together supporters from all teams as we cheered on the national heroes. For us, none came bigger than Bobby Charlton. To say that Bobby single handedly took England to the World Cup final might be an exaggeration, but his two wondrous goals against Portugal in the semi final were magnificent.

The first football song I remember was high up the charts at the time. It was called World Cup Willie by Lonnie Donegan and his skiffle band. In retrospect it was awful, but that didn't stop us singing it all day long as we progressed through the groups, the semi, and onto the final. Playing the World Cup on home soil gave England a massive advantage and the anticipation of winning it for the first time was nationwide. This was the first opportunity for the nation to overcome the sadness of the Munich Air Disaster. Who knows, with Tommy Taylor, Duncan Edwards and Roger Byrne alongside the other England greats in 1958 in Sweden and 1962 in Chile, we could have been going for a third world cup in a row. Sadly, we will never know.

The final itself was a momentous occasion. Every household in England gathered around their televisions in anticipation. The game was a beauty, ebbing and flowing like a tidal river. England took the lead, then Germany scored twice. In the dying moments of normal time, Bobby Moore, the England captain was felled and quickly took a free kick. Goal, England was level. Extra time was a real nail biter until Geoff Hurst scored a beauty, at least that's how the Russian linesman saw it.

Television replays have since showed the ball never crossed the line. In many business dealings with the Germans over the years, I've often longed for a Russian linesman! In the final moments, Geoff Hurst charged forward again, a few fans were on the pitch and Ken Wolstenholme, the famous commentator of the time, shouted into his microphone " There's people on the pitch, they think it's all over – It is now" as Hurst banged it into the net to claim a hat trick and victory for England. I remember screaming too. Four Two against the Germans was a great result and one that should have been the start of several World Cup wins, rather than the ifs and buts we have suffered since.

Some West Ham fans have been known to claim how West Ham won the World Cup because Geoff Hurst and Martin Peters scored the goals in the final and Bobby Moore was the captain. My response has always been that if it wasn't for Bobby Charlton, we wouldn't have got past the first round. That argument usually ends in a tie.

My favourite memory of that final, notwithstanding the greatness of victory, was seeing a toothless Nobby Stiles dancing a jig around Wembley stadium, socks rolled to the ankle. Another United legend going down in the folklore of the game.

The second World Cup final took place later that day on Westminster Street. No fear of Mad Billy or his carnivorous dog spoiling these celebrations. I scored the winning goal too, or at least that's what my memory keeps reminding me.

The 67 Title and New Hope

After the disappointments of 1966, United started the following season with renewed determination. That determination was doubled by the desire to get back into Europe. Winning the European Cup had become the Holy Grail for Matt Busby and United. Before they could compete again for the European Cup, United had to firstly become Champions of England.

For the thin blonde haired kid in Swinton, winning the European Cup was marginally more important than getting into the Cub Scout football team. I had joined the 9th Swinton group mainly to play football but was disappointed because there were so many bigger and older boys in the pack. It was the beginning of my regular starting position of substitute, freezing and never getting a game, while my older pack mates struggled through the mud at Beech Farm playing fields. Apparently a young kid called Ryan Wilson started his career on the same patch of mud and puddles a few years later. That was before he changed his name to Giggs.

Down the road at Old Trafford, United were totally focused on winning the league. This was helped in part by early exits from the FA and League Cups at the hands of Norwich and Blackpool respectively. In the league, United got off to a flyer with George Best as good as ever after recovering from injury. On 20th August, we battered West Brom, going 5-1 up in the first twenty minutes before easing off to let the visitors score a couple of late goals. Five goals to three had set the marker for the season. Going forward, United were unstoppable with Best and Law unplayable. Bobby

Charlton and Nobby Stiles were marshalling the team with the class expected of the World Champions they had become. Unfortunately, they were not as solid at the back, with a defence leaking like a sieve. Busby had to act and he did, bringing in Alex Stepney, the Chelsea goalkeeper. I've read Stepney's autobiography and he was overwhelmed when he first joined United. The size of the club and the expectations were massive compared to his previous club, even though Chelsea was a rival for the title under the management of the peerless Tommy Docherty. Another change was the introduction of a new winger called John Aston, son of a father of the same name who had played for United's title winning team prior to the Busby Babes. Aston junior had a fairly short career at United but it was very effective and we will talk about him in detail shortly.

Live football was not often televised in those days, we had to listen to the radio on match days and then two highlights shows. Match of the Day on the BBC was shown every Saturday night and I was lucky enough to be allowed to stay up to watch it. On Sunday afternoon, Granada showed the Big Match and being local to Manchester, we regularly had the United game as the main feature.

On Saturday nights I would often play Subbeteo table football with Pie and Lionegg before walking to the local chippy for a regular Saturday supper of chips and gravy. We would then return to one of our houses to play the final game of Subbuteo before going our separate ways to watch Match of the Day. The good news is that age and size made no difference to Subbuteo and I would usually win.

I was really getting into the football now and the highlight of the week was Match of the Day. Towards the end of the season, United were televised as the top game more often than not, steaming towards their seventh title that would enable them to chase European glory again. The season was a close one with United and Liverpool swapping top spot several times before United opened up a small gap in April. On the last day of the season a win against West Ham would guarantee the title. In typically swashbuckling style we demolished West Ham at Upton Park 6-1. While others had faltered, United went from strength to strength, eventually winning the league by four points from nearest rivals Nottingham Forest. The continent was back on the horizon.

Busby was later heard to say that Alex Stepney had made the difference and he surely played his part, but the Trinity of Best, Law and Charlton, ably supported by Crerand, Stiles and Foulkes were without peers. United played their football with a style and buzz befitting the greatest club in the world. Just as in 1958 before that fateful day in February, the future looked really bright.

Champions of Europe

United could and perhaps should have been celebrating a magnificent double in 1968 but after dominating the league for most of the season, we faltered at the last hurdle, eventually losing out to local rivals Manchester City by two points. Perhaps it was the extra efforts required in Europe that had taken its toll, perhaps it was the size of the squad, tiring as the games piled up; perhaps it was just City's year. The fact is, that although City won the league, United were still making all the headlines.

The season had started magnificently with a charity shield game at Old Trafford on 12th August. Although the game finished 3-3 and honours were even with Tottenham, the Cup Winners, I shall always remember it for the goal that to this day I still believe is the greatest ever. Stepney rolled the ball out to Tony Dunne in the left back position. He immediately played it down the line to Dennis Law, who sold his marker an outrageous dummy before releasing a young Brian Kidd in the left wing position. Kidd cut inside and played a careful ball into Bobby Charlton who hit the ball, left foot and first time from about twenty five yards. The shot was so ferocious that the ball was still rising as it almost tore the net off the goal posts. The goal was so good that commentator Ken Wolstenholme remarked "That's a goal good enough to win the league, the cup, the charity shield, the world cup and even the Grand National." I love that goal and I loved Ken Wolstenholme, the best commentator ever and not smug like a number of his successors. The fact that he was born in Worsley, just a couple of miles from where I grew up in Swinton, may have been part of the reason.

Wostenholme was a lifelong Bolton fan but you could never tell. His enthusiasm for the game was infectious and his commentary was never biased.

Busby was once again blooding youngsters and as well as eighteen year old Brian Kidd, who replaced an aging David Herd who never recovered from a terrible broken leg, and Johnny Aston whom I mentioned earlier, he also introduced a twenty three year old David Sadler, who seemed able to play in any position, and young full back Francis Burns, another eighteen year old.

In Europe, United made steady progress before reaching the semi finals where they were once again matched against Real Madrid. This time though, United were confident they could beat the six time winners.

I know I promised to talk about real events and not ifs and buts, but I must deviate from that promise for a moment. Had the Babes survived and grown from strength to strength, how many European Cups might they have won. Real may have the silverware, but as always, the glory is still with United.

The first leg of the semi final was at Old Trafford. United had the best of the early exchanges with Paddy Crerand hitting the post. By now, John Aston had made the left wing position his own, with Best on the right. A mesmerizing run by Aston ended with an inch perfect pass to Best who scored the only goal of a pulsating game, sending United to Madrid with a slender advantage.

Dennis Law missed the rest of the season with a knee injury and David Sadler replaced him for the second leg, proving the versatility of this talented player. The records state that 125,000 were packed into the Bernabau that night. Real threw everything at United and raced into an early two goal lead, before an own goal gave United some hope. Just on the stroke of half time, Real scored again, and we were 3-1 down at the interval. It remained that way for the next thirty minutes but then hope! Best found Sadler who scored. Time moved on and then, of all people, Bill Foulkes scored the equalizer. United were through to the final, 4-3 on aggregate.

The final in 1968 was played at Wembley in front of 100,000. If everybody who claimed to have been there had really been there, the attendance would have been closer to a million. Suffice to say, the curly haired eight year old from Swinton was only at Wembley in Spirit.

It was a great game and of course everybody knows that United won 4-1 against the mighty Benfica. But there were a couple of cameos that made the difference. First of all, John Aston played the game of his life. Up and down the wing he went in a tireless and brilliant display of wing play. Secondly, the save made by Alex Stepney with just a couple of minutes to go was as good as I have ever seen. Benfica had equalized late in the game and it looked to be fizzling out towards extra time. A long pass found Eusebio, the brilliant Portugese forward who volleyed the ball towards goal. Stepney not only saved it but caught it as well. The sight of Eusebio applauding Stepney for the save confirmed the legendary status he had, not just as a player but as a man. That save won United the European Cup because in extra time it was all United, scoring three times with Best, Kidd, on his nineteenth birthday, and Charlton scoring his second of the game.

Ten years after the horrors of Munich and United were the first English Champions of Europe.

A Ten Year Old Standing On The Stretford End

I did manage to get to see the Red Devils at Wembley in the cup final. Unfortunately it was Salford Rugby League Club who lost 11-6 to Castleford. United became known as the Red Devils when Matt Busby heard it used as the nickname for their local Rugby League neighbours. He thought the 'nasty' devil would make other teams fear United.

By the end of the 1960's the devil motif was added to the club programmes and scarves before being added to the club badge in 1970.

Busby had a legendary attention to detail and memory. In George Best's biography he tells of the great man not only remembering his father's name when he met him a few years later, but also what he enjoyed to drink.

Seeing Salford at Wembley was a bit surreal because I was a Swinton Lions fan. The Lions had been a great team playing in a great stadium at Station Road in Swinton. All the international matches at the time seemed to be played at Swinton, together with cup semi finals and other important games. I remember standing in the Barn at the Station Road end of the ground watching greats like Kenny Gowers and Alan Buckley. Sadly, Swinton are now a lower league club without a home. The famous old Station Road stadium was sold to developers and has been a housing estate for the last twenty years.

On the field, United were having a real go at retaining the European Cup and at becoming the first English team to become World Champions, a fete they did eventually achieve some 30 odd years later. The World Club Championship was played against Estudiantes over two legs, the first in Argentina and the second at Old Trafford. It was ugly. George Best and Bobby Charlton were kicked off the park, forcing Nobby to deck one of the Argentine players in the centre circle, it was a hell of a right hook as I recall. United lost the game 2-1 on aggregate and Busby remarked afterwards that the Europeans needed to educate their South American counterparts how to play the game. The referees gave United no support and it took its toll. They would eventually finish 11th in the league that season. In Europe, United reached the semi finals and were favorites to retain their trophy. Unfortunately, fate reared its ugly head again. United lost the first leg against AC Milan 2-0. The second leg, at Old Trafford, was a constant bombardment on the Milan goal. Fabio Cudicini, the Milan keeper played the game of his life and seventy frustrating minutes passed before the breakthrough, thanks to a fine run from Best who released Charlton for a typically brilliant finish. A few moments later and Law equalized, the ball clearing the goal line by a yard before a valiant Milan defender scooped it clear. The stadium bounced, Law turned to salute the fans but Mr. Magoo, who had been given the whistle for the game, didn't see it. United, not for the first time, nor the last, were robbed of European glory.

Injury had prevented Dennis Law from playing in the 1968 European Cup Final. This time it was an appalling decision by the referee. One of the greatest players in the history of the game was denied the chance to play in a dream final.

I did get to Old Trafford at last in 1970. It was for an FA Cup replay between non league Wigan Athletic and Port Vale. In those days, if a tie had to go to a second replay, it was played on a neutral ground and the teams elected to play at the Theatre of Dreams. I was amongst a modest crowd, standing on the Stretford End with my friend Ian O'Connell (Conner to his mates) and Brian, his dad and part time Wigan fan. Port Vale won the tie 1-0 in extra time but the experience of being at Old Trafford for the first time was amazing.

When Love Is Not Enough – Poor Old Wilf

Shortly after the European Cup triumph, Matt Busby became Sir Matt Busby, knighted by the Queen for bravery and for services to football. He had built three great United teams, fate robbing us of perhaps the greatest team ever, before they even reached their prime. He retired from the game in 1971, winning the league title five times, the FA Cup twice, and of course the European Cup. Prior to that, he temporarily retired in 1969, at the end of the season.

By the summer of 1969 I was playing football almost every day. Some of my friends played cricket in the summer but not me, at least not if I could help it. I'd now graduated from perpetual substitute for the cub team to right half, which today is of course right midfield. I was also amongst a group of boys at Mossfield Junior School who were good enough to beat the school team, picked of boys from the year above us. I also got rid of my first pair of cheap boots and inherited Pie's Adidas La Paz boots. I loved those boots.

In the late sixties and early seventies, there were a number of boys' comics that focused on football. Roy of the Rovers featured in Tiger, there was Score n Roar and my personal favorite – Scorcher. I would receive Scorcher through the letter box every Saturday morning and read it from cover to cover in front of the fire with a bowl of cornflakes. There were some great features in Scorcher like Paxton's Powerhouses, a team with a mad coach and nutty professor who would use really weird experiments and science to make the team invincible. There was the Kangaroo Kid from Australia who could jump ten feet in the air to volley a ball. Strange that, as most Aussie footballers I have seen can't even jump high enough to get a beer mat under their studs. (Tim Cahill being a credible exception.) My favorite player though was Billy Dane who featured in the wonderful story of Billy's Boots. Billy Dane was never very good at football until he inherited an old pair of boots that had once belonged to the world famous striker – 'Dead Shot Keen'. Once Billy put the boots on, he was as good as Keen and became an unstoppable player. Whether this was by magic, or by some kind of psychological boost, I don't know. All I know is that when Billy played in those boots, he was a marvel. It seemed that Pie's old boots had the same effect on me, and remember that he was three years older. Suddenly I believed I was as good as any twelve year old on the planet. It was a shame that none of my mates had the same opinion.

Back at the Theatre of Dreams, Matt had recommended Wilf McGuiness to succeed him and the board agreed. Wilf was only 31 at the time and had been with the club since a junior at the time of the Babes. His age and lack of experience ultimately went against him, that and the impossible task of following Sir Matt Busby. As a player, Wilf had been unlucky when a series of injuries forced his early retirement. The one great story I remember about Wilf shows his diligence and commitment to succeed. When Wilf was breaking into the first team, it was dominated by right footed players and Wilf himself was a right half. His reaction wasn't to mope or ask for a transfer or demand a chance. At the end of every training session, Wilf would spend hours kicking and controlling a ball against a wall at the Cliff training ground, using only his left foot. When Wilf eventually became a regular, everybody thought he was a natural left footer.

As manager, Wilf struggled because many of the players regarded him as a peer, rather than the new boss. The team was inconsistent and flirted relegation for a while before eventually finishing off the pace in eighth place. Even though they reached the semi finals of the FA Cup and League Cup, Wilf was relieved of his duties and Sir Matt took temporary charge of the team.

Wilf McGuiness was Manchester United through and through, his dedication as a player proved that. He was unlucky as a manager, and maybe not given enough time. Following Busby was the greatest challenge anybody could face. There was another problem that has had little press over the years. Many of the players felt they had achieved everything in the game after beating Benfica at Wembley. George Best has said on more than one occasion that he felt there was no ambition in the dressing room. No wonder Wilf failed, despite his total love of Manchester United. He did get a couple of other managers jobs after that but you could see his heart was still at Old Trafford. He also lost all his hair as a result of the stress and the pressure of running the Worlds' biggest club.

Wilf is sometimes seen on MUTV today, and adds occasional articles on the Manutd.com web page. They are always worth a read and Wilf is still a top man that I'd love to have a beer with.

Farewell Bobby

Everybody in the world who has an opinion about Sir Bobby Charlton has written about him. Bobby is a gentleman and one of the best English players ever to lace up his boots.

I was lucky enough to see him play a few times before he retired and the most amazing thing to me was his pace. Bobby is well remembered for his shooting and passing ability with either foot, but I can't ever remember him being beaten for pace by anybody. Bobby had an awareness about him that only Paul Scholes has been able to match. People say that he was so well respected that nobody in England ever kicked him. That's a load of rubbish. The reason he was never kicked was because nobody could get near him. Bobby Charlton could find space anywhere, control the ball immediately and then pass it to a team mate without thinking. He didn't make many tackles because his mind and feet were so quick and so much in sync, that he could nip the ball away from an opponent without the need to fly in.

From 1970 to 1973, nothing of any note was really happening on the field for United. Matt would eventually retire for good in 1971 after Wilf had failed to succeed him. During the period, all we had to show was three 8th place finishes in the league. In 1971, Frank O'Farrell took over the reins and the Stretford End soon found new words to the old 'Roll Out The Barrel' song. Unfortunately for Frank, when the early promise turned into more disappointment for an expectant band of reds, the words were changed again and not in a complimentary way.

The team was not improving and O'Farrell made a couple of signings to freshen things up. The first, a really classy looking defender called Martin Buchan from Aberdeen. Buchan easily stood out in the United line up because apart from Bobby Charlton, who had no hair saving a thin wisp that ran down the side of his face. Buchan had an unfashionable short but smart haircut. In the early seventies, teenagers and young men often had longer hair than their female counterparts. The United players were no exception. Despite his smart appearance and clean shaven face, Buchan settled in quickly and shored up the leaky defence.

The other signing was Ian Storey Moore from Nottingham Forest. Story-Moore excited me as a player, he was quick, strong and skilful. Unfortunately he was also injury prone and we never saw the best of him, despite a promising start. With Charlton and Law past their peak, Brian Kidd failing to live up to the early promise and Best spending more time suspended than playing, we were in trouble.

A word or two about Best here. Apart from one glorious performance in the FA Cup against Northampton, following a six week ban, Best never again dominated football. He was still in his mid twenties when he scored six goals that day but he was spending more time outside the game than in it. He would miss training, not even turning up on some occasions, and his fame, fortune, good looks and obvious charm, made him a prime target for the ladies. Best dated three Miss World's, and he once joked on a Michael Parkinson Show that it would have been five but he didn't turn up for two of them. The Belfast boy was now controlled by alcohol and the weight piled on him. We still loved him but did he still love himself? What a waste of an amazing talent.

My career was starting to take off too. In 1970 my sister was born. In those days we didn't have scans to determine the sex of the baby and I'd spent weeks cleaning my old football boots for her and designing training programmes to teach her all I knew about the game. Of course, as she grew up she had little interest in playing, but she remains a red to this day and unlike me, has always lived in Swinton. I was now the captain of the 9th Swinton cub team but more importantly, I was playing for Mossfield Junior School.

I started at Right back but liked going forward much more than defending and soon graduated to right half. My mate Connor, who I'd been to Old Trafford with, was centre forward and Smicker was the left half. The pacey Stephen Blackburn or Blackie played right wing and Andrew Sheard was centre half. Nobody got past Sheardy. Chris Scott sometimes played alongside him but often played in goal. Scotty was so good in goal that he became a wicketkeeper, playing as first choice for Lancashire for a number of years.

We swept all before us that year but for me it was a mixed blessing. Towards the end of the season I developed appendicitis and missed the last few games, including the Cup Final. I did, however go camping with the cubs on the same weekend of the Final and played in a camp tournament, scoring a hat trick in the final. Mr. Straw, my teacher at Mossfield was good enough to get me a cup medal, and so that season I received three winners' medals. 1971 was the second best treble season ever.

Mr. Straw was a Manchester City fan but despite that he really liked me, even when I bought a pair of Stylo Matchmaker football boots. These boots were the most amazing thing with a flap across the laces, but they looked much better than they performed. They were also made exclusively with George Best's name attached, the first football sponsorship that I remember. Mr. Straw once commented that he hoped I played better than George Best, fat chance that anybody could ever do that! Best was as brave as a lion as well as being superbly gifted. Some of his goals are totally unforgettable. Like the lob across a crowded penalty box against Tottenham and when he robbed Eddy McCready of Chelsea before chipping a bewildered goalkeeper from an impossible angle.

Personal success for me at Mossfield barely made up for the dismal proceedings at Old Trafford and at the end of 1972, Frank O'Farrell was dismissed. Three years on and United still hadn't managed to replace Busby.

Eventually Tommy Docherty arrived from Chelsea. The Doc was a larger than life character and he made sweeping changes to the club he called the greatest in football.

He soon fell out with George Best, declaring that nobody was bigger than the club and he controversially let Dennis Law go to Manchester City for a free transfer.

At the end of the 1973 season, Bobby Charlton hanged up his boots for the last time, retiring after 754 games for United, scoring 247 goals. He was also capped 106 times for England and scored 49 goals. His goal scoring achievements for United and England are still records to this day. I talked about the greatest goal ever that Charlton scored but he scored many other beauties too. One goal he scored at Anfield was fired in from the corner of the penalty area and was still rising when it hit the net about three feet off the ground.

Bobby Charlton was European footballer of the year in 1966, Dennis Law had previously been crowned King of Europe in 1964 and then in 1968 it was George Best. In the nineteen sixties United consistently fielded a team with three European footballers of the year. Now in the early seventies they had all gone. Tommy Docherty had a huge job on his hands.

Shortly after retiring, the Queen rewarded Bobby with a knighthood. Sir Bobby Charlton flirted with management for a couple of seasons but soon returned to Old Trafford as a football ambassador, where he has remained ever since.

The Worst Year of Our Lives

At the end of the 1973 season, United finished 18th, barely avoiding relegation. With Bobby retired, Dennis at Maine Road, and George spending more and more time away from The Cliff, we were not optimistic. But United were still the biggest club in the world and far too good to face another barren year.

I was enjoying some of my best football, now at Wardley Grammar school. We were a small school with fewer boys to choose from than the other schools in the area, but we held our own and several of us were watched by lower division teams like Blackburn Rovers and Bolton Wanderers. I always got the same response – too thin and weak. No wonder my mates were calling me 'Twiggy' at the time. It never stopped me trying though and I was a box to box midfielder (at least that's what my memory is telling me).

Being as thin as a rake, I often got hurt on the muddy fields we played on, prompting my mother to advise me to focus more on golf, a game I'd started to play with my old mate Connor. All we had was Connor's dad's half set of Presidential Clubs. We shared them between five or six of us, and we quickly converted Beech Farm playing fields into our golf course. Connor had been playing for a while and could hit the ball a fair distance and in the air. I was still occasionally missing with an air shot. Finally the big day was arriving, a first outing at Bolton Municipal Golf Course and we charged down to Beech Farm for a last day of practice. Connor shouted fore at the top of his lungs and I turned round to see which unlucky blighter the ball was heading towards. As I turned it felt like a howitzer smashed into my face, just below the nose, just above the teeth. When I came round, my two front teeth were loose but miraculously not broken and my nose was all over my face. Thanks Mum for advising me to take up a safe sport like golf. That was the worst facial injury I've ever had.

Next day we still went to Bolton Municipal, with a broken nose, two re-set teeth, two black eyes and a top lip as thick as a Cumberland sausage, I was ready. Anything within a yard of the hole was a gimme and there were approximately twenty mulligans each for Connor and I. However, I actually managed to birdie the last hole, a short par three. My carded score of 102 hid the real 120 or so it should have been, but nobody can ever take away that first real birdie on my first real game of golf.

Playing football and golf were the only two respites from another appalling United season. We didn't have much money as a family and my only job was a paper round, so I rarely got to Old Trafford. The Doc had introduced some new blood but our fate was hopeless. The last few games were nerve-racking for us, and a joy to the few City fans we had at Wardley. Each day we would bring in our newspapers to read before school started, then we'd start looking at the points scored and the points needed. Then we figured out who we had to beat to stay up and how many points we thought we would end the season with. Unanimously, we believed we would stay up. We were obviously using a primitive version of Michael Essiens' calculator because the actual score didn't match our predictions. In April 1974 we went into the penultimate game of the season, knowing that we had to win and Birmingham lose or draw for us to stay in the top flight. Who were we playing? Our opponents were Manchester City, with a certain Dennis Law playing as their main striker. With only a few minutes left, an innocuous Francis Lee cross found Dennis with his back to goal, he instinctively (and half heartedly) back heeled the ball in the direction of the goal. Somehow it went through a crowd of players into the net. As the City players ran towards Dennis, you could see how terrible he felt, he was almost in tears. One of those City players was a real hero of the blue half of Manchester. Mike Doyle hated United with a passion, and we felt the same about him. You'd have thought Doyle had won the world cup the way he celebrated. As for Dennis, he didn't celebrate the goal and he never played again. Like Pat Crerand and Wilf McGuiness before him, Dennis was United through and through and is still a regular on MUTV.

As it happened, Birmingham beat Norwich and the result at Old Trafford was irrelevant. United were relegated. The classroom at Wardley almost flooded in the tears of broken-hearted teenagers.

The Doc's New Team and New Hope

The 1974/75 season kicked off with everybody, especially the fans, determined to head straight back into the top flight. The Docs new team was to say the least, small. We had Gordon Hill and Stevie Coppell flying down the wings, added together they weighed about the same as your average sized puppy. In central midfield was Gerry Daly, an Irishman that made me look fat, and Sammy McIlroy, the last ever Busby Babe who had been signed as a schoolboy from Northern Ireland. Up front, a swashbuckling Stuart (Pancho) Pearson and 'Skip to My' Lou Macari. Macari was about four feet tall (or so it seemed) but he was amazing in the air. He could jump like The Kangaroo Kid. Despite the size of the team, they were tenacious and very exciting to watch.

The fans seemed to sing all through every match with United Road trying to out-sing the Stretford End and vice versa. More than fifty thousand were crammed into every home game and I remember seeing the look on the faces of the lowly York City players as they came through the tunnel.

When we beat Sunderland 3-2 at Old Trafford in November 1974, in front of more than sixty thousand fans with thousands more outside, we were 6 points clear. The exception to the miniature size rule was an uncompromising Scottish centre half called Jim Holton. Alongside the clever and stylish Martin Buchan he was colossal, prompting the Stretford End to sing 'Six Foot Two, Eyes of Blue, Big Jim Holton's after you.' Sadly, later that season he broke his leg in a 4-4 draw at Sheffield Wednesday and never recovered.

Old Trafford in those days was by far the biggest ground in the country, but it wasn't all ticket. Apart from about 30,000 season ticket holders, the rest of us got into the ground on a first come first served basis. People would start to queue outside their favorite parts of the ground at noon. That's a staggering three hours before the kick off. The Stretford End, lower reaches of United Road, Stretford Paddock and the lower half of the Scoreboard End were terraced and fans would stand. Most of the time this was great, but occasionally you'd be near a few really drunk hoodlums and you can imagine what they would be like. In fact, you'll have to use your imagination because I want this book to be a family read, but sometimes it was very ugly.

I was in my final couple of years at Wardley by now and the dreaded O'Levels were looming. As a team we were still fighting well above our weight and made it through to the Quarter Finals of The Greater Manchester Cup. On one occasion, we played a team from Chevington, near Wigan, and they had a couple of lads who had signed junior forms with Liverpool. Their Headmaster was so convinced his team would win the trophy that he gave the whole school the afternoon off to watch us play, providing they agreed to watch and not skive off home. The game was electric and I remember getting a couple of kicks from the supporters when I chased a ball for a throw in. We drew 4-4 and had the privilege of taking them back to Wardley. We begged Mr. Jenkinson our Headmaster to return the favour but all he consented to was letting us kick off a half hour before the school day closed and to ask the school to come out and support us. It worked, we had about forty people watching, that's more than any previous home game but still less than ten per cent the size of the Chevington crowd. I remember them going a goal up, I equalized, then in the second half we banged in three more to win 4-1. Those two games were the best I played in at school. In the next round we were hammered 5-1 at home by a school from Prestwich. They seemed to have more players on the field than us and it was only after the game had ended that I found out our right back, Dave Fitton, had been sent off in the first half. The dream was over.

As I was getting older I was given more freedom and remember going to a travelling fair at the back of the Embankment at Swinton Rugby Ground. It was a great night with lots of flirting with some of the pretty young girls of Swinton, but on the way home I got jumped by five lads and my recently re-built nose was now flattened across my face again. I owe my rugged good looks to a golf ball and a few thugs.

At Old Trafford, United were still playing incredible football and still averaging over 50,000 for home games. It was no surprise when we stormed straight back to the top flight. The Docs team of pint sized geniuses had the character and skill to stay on top of the second division throughout, eventually finishing as second division champions ahead of runners-up, Aston Villa. United were back.

The following season was amazing and if United had been a bit luckier, and had a bigger squad, we might have been celebrating a famous double. The team played with the same care-free style that had dominated the second division. Eventually we ran out of steam. An unlikely defeat at home to Stoke meant we finished third in the league. In the FA Cup, United played Derby in the semi final, after brushing all aside, and two Gordon Hill goals put United through. Gordon was at last living up to his Stretford End billing as the king of all cockneys. The 1976 final was played against second division Southampton and the bookies had United as clear favorites. We peppered the Saints goal but with seven minutes left, Jim McCalliog, another one of Docherty's United outcasts found Bobby Stokes. He ran past two defenders to score a fine goal in the corner. I may be biased but to this day I believe Stokes was offside. The linesman disagreed and the record books show a 1-0 win to Southamption. It was a disappointing end to a very good season, but the future again looked bright for the Red Devils.

Cookes, Swinton Town and Old Traffordians

Shortly after the FA Cup final in 1976 I left Wardley and looked forward to starting work as a technician apprentice with GEC Switchgear in Trafford Park. Now I would be able to walk to Old Trafford for night games after work, and afford to go to games on a Saturday.

I needed a team to play for and thanks to an unusual connection through a friend of a friend, I joined Cookes Sports Football Club. Cookes was a sports shop in the centre of Manchester and the manager of the football section was also the manager of the team. We played on Sunday mornings in the Blackley League. It was exciting playing against men, but also a bit scary for a scrawny sixteen year old. Some teams would gladly trade their skills for a good fight. It kept me in shape though and enabled me to move on when the time was right. One story I will share is when we played The Embassy Club. For those who don't know, The Embassy Club was owned by Manchester comedian Bernard Manning. Manning was one of the rudest and crudest comedians around but was exceptionally funny. He was a devout City fan who also spent his Sunday mornings cheering on his Embassy team. When we played them, at Boggart Hole Clough. (I kid you not. There is a large municipal park called 'Boggart Hole Clough,' which is bordered by Moston and Blackley. Clough is a northern dialect word for a steep sided, wooded valley; a large part of Boggart Hole Clough is made up of these valleys and is said to be inhabited by Boggarts. A Boggart is a household spirit which causes things to disappear, milk to sour, and dogs to go lame. Supposedly mysterious disappearances would occur, particularly in the early 19th century, where these mysteries were often attributed to the Boggart of the Clough. Fans of Harry Potter may recognize the term Boggart.) Anyway, Cookes' team had the dubious privilege of playing home games there.

The winter had set in and the central sections of the field were wet and muddy. My lightweight frame meant that I was often asked to play on the wing. Usually this was a blessing and I was fairly quick. Against The Embassy Club I was matched against an aging full back who obviously enjoyed a beer and he couldn't get near me or the ball. After I'd beaten him for countless times I heard a famous voice shout out, 'Will somebody kick this cocky little bxxxxxds fxxxxng legs off.' I didn't get my legs kicked off, but I did shy away from the ball. Manning left the game in his giant Cadillac before the final whistle; with a grin on his face. I never saw him again but I don't suppose that bothered him.

Shortly afterwards, my friend Smicker invited me to join him at Swinton Town FC. This was a mixed blessing because on the one hand, it was a good standard of football, but on the other, the games were played on a Saturday afternoon, keeping me away from Old Trafford again. I enjoyed playing for Swinton but it was short lived because the team folded a season after I joined them.

I was working for GEC Switchgear in Trafford Park, and while Swinton Town was folding, the inter-department competition began. I was asked to play for the department and although we lost, the manager asked if I'd be interested in playing for him at Old Traffordians in the Lancashire and Cheshire League. Now this was a step in the right direction and I leapt at the chance. I stayed with Old Traffordians until I was twenty one when torn ankle ligaments halted my playing. The ankle injury meant I could once again spend my Saturdays at Old Trafford watching the greatest team in the world, but more of that later.

When Love is Too Much

The disappointment of the 1976 FA Cup final gave United a real determination to win a trophy the following season. The Doc had promised silverware and we all believed him.

Away from football, my golf game was suffering after discovering the pleasures of beer and noticing that girls actually are okay. My first pint was in The Golden Lion on Bolton Road in Clifton. It was a pint of Chester's Dark Mild. I got confident and although only seventeen, I was able to act and look mature enough to get served in most pubs. My favorite pub at that time was the Nadgers, or Albert Inn to give its' formal name. The Nadgers sold Boddingtons, that's the real deal hand pulled stuff, not this dreadful excuse for a beer we get in draught-flow cans today. We would usually stop in the Nadgers for 2 or three pints on our way to the Duke of Wellington for the Friday Night disco.

I hated Disco music with a passion but the girls all loved it so what was I to do on a Friday? On one occasion, a friend of a friend joined us in the Nadgers. This guy looked about ten years old and when he asked for a pint, the barman said 'A pint of what?' The kids' reply of a pint of beer got us all thrown out for underage drinking. Next week he had a passport as proof of his age, he was actually 19 years old.

Another off field activity was attending concerts by the best rock bands of the time. I saw Bad Company, Sad Café and Jethro Tull in one year and Black Sabbath (yes with Ozzie) and Uriah Heep in another year. My dream to see Led Zeppelin live would have to wait as they were making millions on tour in the USA at the time.

On television, and we now had the luxury of three channels and several programmes in colour, we had the brilliant Monty Pythons Flying Circus and every Christmas The Morecambe and Wise Show. One of my favorites at the time was the bungling magician and comedian, Tommy Cooper. Tommy would make me laugh just by walking on to the stage. Once a year on the television we would be treated to the Royal Variety Show. This was where the top artists of the day would be invited to perform in front of the Queen and other members of the Royal Family. At the end of the show, all the artists would meet the Queen for a quick thank you as she headed off back to the palace. The legend that is Tommy Cooper allegedly had the following conversation:

"Excuse me Ma'am, do you like football?"

"No Mr. Cooper, not really." Her Majesty replied.

"Can I have your tickets for the Cup Final?" Tommy quipped.

In the seventies the FA Cup was usually presented to the captain of the winning team by the Queen.

The brave but ultimately disappointing 1976 season had revived our optimism at Old Trafford. The third place finish put us back into Europe and we eased our way past Ajax in the first round of the UEFA Cup. The swashbuckling naivety of our style though came undone and we were narrowly beaten by an exceptional Juventus side in the second round. Our league performances were a bit of a rollercoaster ride too. We were out of running for the title by Christmas, allowing us to totally focus on the FA Cup.

We got our own back on Southampton on our way to a memorable final. The old token system received on the Match Day United programme meant that occasional visitors to Old Trafford like me had no chance of getting to the Cup Final. So I had to settle down to watch the game on TV. United played Liverpool who were chasing an unprecedented treble of League, European Cup and FA Cup. We were the only thing in their way and we just had to beat them. But on paper they were so powerful and the scousers were rightly confident. Beating Liverpool that day remains one of my favorite memories. A brilliant Stuart Pearson goal broke the deadlock on fifty minutes. Almost immediately they had equalized. The scouse tails were up now and we all feared the worst. Then, Lou Macari and Jimmy Greenhoff conspired to score the freakiest goal in Cup Final history. Lou headed the ball towards Greenhoff who challenged the Liverpool defence. The ball bounced awkwardly to Macari who swung a leg towards it. The shot would have gone wide had it not hit Jimmy in the midriff and spin over a hapless Ray Clemence into the goal. We held on for a memorable win, our first FA Cup since 1963.

I celebrated with a few friends that night, discovering both the fun and dangers of a pub crawl. I got no sympathy from my parents the following day but we had won the Cup so who cares? It all cleans up, and the smell fades, eventually.

A huge crowd filled Albert Square outside Manchester Town Hall to greet our heroes on their victory parade. Tommy Docherty's passionate speech declared, "We promised you last year that we would bring the cup back. And we have brought the cup back – To the finest supporters in the world." We absolutely loved The Doc, and he loved us right back. We practiced our pub crawling techniques again, this time with a bit more care. Having a final pint in a pub called Tommy Ducks. Unfortunately Tommy Ducks is no longer there but what a place it was. Hanging from the ceiling were hundreds of pairs of girls knickers.

Nobody could have predicted what happened next. Instead of a number of summer signings to strengthen the team and make a new assault on the title, we lost the Doc. His love affair with Mary Brown, the wife of the clubs physio, became public knowledge and the Doc was sacked. The love of Manchester United had brought Tommy Docherty to Old Trafford; the love of Mary Brown took him away.

Those of us lucky enough to see the Tommy Docherty team in the nineteen seventies have nothing but good memories. Yes we were inconsistent, and we could have done better in the league. But every year was an improvement on the previous and the Doc left us with a great basis for future success.

Dave Sexton

The man charged with the considerable task of keeping the momentum going was Dave Sexton. Sexton was the total opposite of the Doc. He was a quiet reserved man but a brilliant tactician. Sextons approach was more cautious, more defensively aware and with more emphasis on tactics. Unfortunately we often looked a bit confused on the pitch.

Football hooliganism was rife at this time and some of the European police forces seemed to revel in a good fight as much as the hooligans. We played St Etienne in France and the fans got a right good tonking from the French Police who were battering men women and children indiscriminately. UEFA's response was to kick us out of the European Cup Winners Cup. Although we did get that decision reversed we had to play the return leg away from Old Trafford, eventually at Plymouth. We went through but then lost 6-5 over two legs to Porto, ending the European dream for another season.

My visits to Old Trafford were still restricted to night games as I was playing regularly on a Saturday. The early exit from Europe and the Plymouth penalty left me without live football for another season.

We needed to replace the aging Alex Stepney and his long time understudy, Paddy Roche, failed to make the grade. An eager 20 year old South African called Gary Bailey seized his chance and became our number one for a few years. Two early and notable additions to the squad were Joe Jordan and Gordon McQueen, both from Leeds. Big Gordon dominated in the air. My favorite though was Joe Jordan. Joe was an uncompromising

Centre Forward with a lot more skill than he was given credit for. Joe's famous grin, with two front teeth missing from a kick in the face as a young man, was legendary.

One of my team mates at Old Traffordians resembled Joe because his two front teeth were also missing. Gary Wilkinson was more of a winger though than a striker. He had just broken into the first team when I got to know him. He was a good kid but sadly went missing after a night out in Manchester. A few days later his body was found at Pomona Dock on the Manchester Ship Canal. A tragic loss of life and I don't believe the true cause of death was ever known. Although I barely knew him, Gary's death affected me quite badly, especially my desire to play football. When I tore ankle ligaments later that season, I packed in playing for many years.

Sexton's first year in charge was transitional and United finished tenth in the league. The following season was barely any better, finishing ninth but there was a glimmer of hope thanks to a good cup run. United met Arsenal at Wembley in 1979. Although outplayed for much of the game and two nil down approaching the last ten minutes, we never gave up. McQueen scored with four minutes to spare. We had hope. Within a minute, Sammy McIlroy made a sensational run before slotting the ball into the corner of the net. We were level. The Arsenal players heads dropped and they were a spent force. There was just over a minute to go and then extra time, where we would have surely thrashed them. Unfortunately for us, Liam Brady of Arsenal hadn't read the script. In a last ditch attack he beat a couple of defenders before releasing a teammate on the right wing. The winger sent a hopeful ball into the United penalty area. Everybody missed it except Alan Sunderland at the back post. 3-2 to Arsenal was the final score.

That summer I finally got to see Led Zeppelin live. The event was at Knebworth in Hertfordshire and I joined about a thousand Mancunians on the coaches from Piccadilly Gardens in Manchester. We left at midnight and arrived at the venue around six o'clock the following morning. It was a glorious summer day and white skins soon turned pink, then red. The beer was flowing and the atmosphere electric. Amongst the support acts for the all day gig were Fairport Convention, who were brilliant, Todd Rundgren who was pretty good too and Chas and Dave. Now Chas and Dave probably go down really well in a pub or small venue, but in front of 200,000? Finally the long summer day turned to dusk and Zeppelin hit the stage. I was fairly close to the front but nowhere near close enough to see the whites of their eyes. I may be biased but I thought they were magnificent that night, playing for almost four hours and it was close to one o'clock in the morning when we trundled back to the coaches. Actually we trundled back to where the coaches should have been. The drivers had all left, empty. There were a thousand angry Mancunians stranded in Hertfordshire. That wouldn't be the last time that British service and incompetence screwed me. It's about time we turned the famous British stiff upper lip to a few stiff uppercuts if you ask me.

The Cup Run again seemed to fuel a new belief. I for one couldn't wait for the new season to begin, especially as Sexton was promised a few quid to spend on players. A good addition was Ray Wilkins from Chelsea. He was a stylish midfielder who at twenty one was already an England regular. Wilkins provided the control that Sexton was looking for in midfield. The 1980 season started well and it soon developed into a two horse race between United and our fiercest rivals from the other end of the East Lancashire Road. A run of bad form in January and February left us trailing Liverpool by six points. Sexton demanded improvement and we won the next six games, bringing us level on points with the scousers. Unfortunately, we lost the last game and Liverpool won. We finished second, just two points behind our rivals.

The 1980-81 season was by comparison a disaster. Early defeats in all the cups and a measly eighth place in the league was all we had to show. We also wasted a fortune on Garry Birtles who we bought from Nottingham Forest. Garry couldn't stop scoring at Forest, at United he couldn't start. He scored just one goal in twenty eight games. After three years of steady progress the team was again in decline. The worst of it though was the style in which we were playing. United have always been synonymous with attractive attacking football but under Dave Sexton we had become boring. Perhaps he was studying the successes at Leeds and Liverpool who had been winning titles by playing ultra defensively but that would never do at Old Trafford. Dave Sexton left the club at the end of the 1981 season and we needed somebody with a verve and the charisma to put the buzz back into Old Trafford. Enter Big Ron Atkinson.

One concern we had in the Manchester pubs was around rumblings that Jordan wasn't being offered a new contract, the club refusing to bring his pay to parity with other stars. He was sold to AC Milan before being replaced by Frank Stapleton who had scored one of Arsenals goals in the 1979 Cup Final. The sad thing for the fans was that we heard that Frank was offered more per week than Joe had asked for. I would have loved to have seen Joe and Frank terrorizing defences together, so would a lot of other United fans. Sadly, the ones in the know at Old Trafford didn't see it that way. Stapleton was Big Ron's first signing.

Gold, Champagne and Big Ron

The arrival of Big Ron also earmarked my first season as a regular at Old Trafford. The ankle injury was slow to heel and the loss of Gary at Old Traffordians had taken away my desire to play. But it hadn't taken away my love for football in general, and United in particular. Surely the biggest character in football would bring the glory days back.

I had moved to Little Lever at the time and although it is in Bolton, there were as many United fans living in 'the village' as there were Bolton. One of them, Ste Howarth worked in the petrol station where I filled up the car. We became mates through our mutual love of United and I started travelling to Old Trafford with Ste, Mick Jones and big Julian. I never did know Julians' last name but he was as sound as a pound. The other red who sometimes came with us was Chris Bradbury, a nutcase with a heart of gold. They were all Stretford Enders but I preferred United Road. We compromised, spending some games in each enclosure. There were many reasons I liked United Road including the banter of a slightly older group of fans. We were also closer to the away fans and the singing seemed more competitive. The main reason though was that I could always find a way to stand close to the end that United were attacking. I would line up alongside the penalty area that we attacked in each half.

There were lots of reasons to be enthusiastic about the team that Big Ron inherited. Despite their lowly final league position the season before, they had won their last seven games. He was also offered money to spend if the right players became available. After signing Frank from Arsenal he turned his attention to Bryan Robson and broke the British transfer record to bring him to Old Trafford. He also brought in Remi Moses. Both players had been with him at his previous club, West Bromwich Albion. Atkinson remarked on the day he unveiled Robson "There is no gamble paying this money for Bryan Robson, he is solid gold".

On the day that Robson signed for United, on the pitch at Old Trafford, Sammy McIlroy responded with a brilliant hat trick. It wasn't enough to keep him at the club and he was sold to Stoke City. I believe we sold him too early because Sammy still had a lot to offer.

McIlroy was replaced by Arnold Muhren, a Dutchman who had been playing for Ipswich Town. Arnold was one of the smartest players I'd ever seen and completed an amazing midfield of Coppell, Wilkins, Robson and Muhren, with Remi Moses able to slot in as necessary.

Critics of United had long said that our fans don't come from Manchester. You only have to walk around Manchester or visit the local schools to know that the claim is patently untrue. I will admit that we have many more out of town fans than any other club in the world, but that is because we have more fans than any other club in the world. When I was a young boy, the city of Manchester was roughly divided 50/50 with City fans. That has gradually become about 60/40 in Uniteds' favour as the reds go from strength to strength and the blues continue to flatter to deceive. It was about this time that several away fans started to sing "We support our local team." A song that annoyed the Old Trafford faithful as most of us were from Manchester. In response, United Road developed a new song with one simple line aimed at the away fans – "If yer can't talk proper shut yer gob." It was a beautiful retort because if you didn't come from Manchester, you had no idea what it meant. I haven't heard that one for a while but would love it to be resurrected if we can find anybody in the stadium willing to start singing again.

Big Ron's love of life, fine cigars, gold jewelry and champagne reflected in the way to team played. We were back to the beautiful attacking football that was expected of us. Even if on occasion we got a hiding. Unfortunately we weren't scoring enough goals. Frank Stapleton was a great leader of the line but he was never prolific, and Garry Birtles, after silencing his critics for a while, was once again the butt of every stand up comedians' jokes. Big Ron gambled by promoting a youngster from the youth team. Norman Whiteside was an instant success and Garry Birtles disappeared without a trace.

Ron Atkinson's first season in charge saw United finish in third place.

There's Only One Bryan Robson

The 1982/83 season was soon off and running despite the small matter of a World Cup in which England flattered to deceive but Bryan Robson cemented his growing reputation, including scoring a brace against France with the fastest goal in World Cup history and a beautiful second half header. As far as I was concerned, United were much more important than England and I was glad the lads came back unscathed.

We looked invincible as we tore teams apart and going into the Christmas period I was convinced that the long wait for the title was over. Then the wheels fell off. Ray Wilkins broke his cheek bone and missed three months and other key players had niggles. In particular we seemed to have more than our share of hamstring injuries. We eventually finished in third place again.

In the cups we had the small matter of taking on Arsenal, twice. After two great legs in the League Cup semi final, which was now called The Milk Cup thanks to some dubious sponsoring, we were through to face Liverpool at Wembley. This was a game we should have won, we deserved to win, but we lost 2-1. It started brightly with a great goal from Norman Whiteside. Liverpool got a lucky equalizer and it was all to play for. Suddenly United's players started dropping like flies and we were patched up all over the place. Gordon McQueen could barely walk but he stayed on the pitch for nuisance factor. With barely a minute to go and extra time looming, Gordon managed to get some strength and chased onto a long through ball, he nicked it past Bruce Grobbelar the Pool keeper and had a clear run at goal. Grobbelar body checked him off the field.

The rules at the time meant it should have been a straight red card but the referee bottled it. I wondered if he celebrated with the Pool players after the match. He had certainly won them the game.

We were out of touch in the league and so the FA Cup was our last chance of glory. We again faced the mighty Arsenal in the semi final at Villa Park. It didn't look good when the Gunners took an early lead, but Robson and his teammates were made of sterner stuff and we eventually won the game 2-1. The Final should have been a foregone conclusion as we were playing Brighton and Hove Albion. Despite finding their way to the final, Brighton was also being relegated from the top flight. The game itself is a bit of a blur as there were a few beers involved but there are two key moments that anybody who saw it, will remember forever. The first was Ray Wilkins making a forward run, turning the defender inside out and hitting a curling twenty five yarder with his left foot into the corner. That goal made the score 2-1 and it should have been all over for the South coast team. Somehow they managed an equalizer. Then in the dying minutes, Gordon Smith, the Brighton striker found himself clean through and one on one with Gary Bailey. It should have been curtains but Gary made a great save.

The replay was a non event and we ran out 4-0 winners with two goals from Robson, one from Whiteside and an Arnold Muhren penalty. Steve Coppell missed the final but we didn't know at the time that his knee injury would end his career.

The player of the season was Bryan Robson and he was rapidly becoming the golden boy of English football. Robson was fast and brave with a tremendous left foot. He timed his runs into the penalty area to perfection and scored many great headers, often at the end of a move he had started in front of our own penalty area. He wasn't a defensive midfielder, nor an attacking midfielder, he was both and the best player we had seen in the red shirt since the Trinity.

The 1983/84 season was a mixed bag. We never replaced Steve Coppell and often looked un-balanced in midfield.

There was joy in the Carter household though, my son James was born in September, a bouncing 7 lbs lad that was the newest member of the Manchester United family, even if he didn't yet know it.

United did manage fourth in the league but early and embarrassing exits from the domestic cups at the hands of Oxford and Bournemouth had all our rivals laughing at us. The only respite came in the European Cup Winners Cup where we had unconvincingly found our way to the quarter final where we would take on the mighty Barcelona. Some Argentinean called Diego Maradona played for the Catalan giants, alongside Berndt Schuster, the superstar of German football. It didn't look good when we lost the first leg at the Nou Camp 2-0, despite some resolute defending.

I left work early and queued outside the Stretford End for what seemed like hours in the rain. Nobody wanted to miss this game. I had no idea where any of my mates were but didn't care. This was going to be one hell of a game of football. When I eventually got in, the left side of the tunnel, where I normally stood, was already overcrowded, the right side was barely any better. We were squashed like sardines and soaking wet. Could we do it?

The game started and the first United attack was met with an almighty rush from the back of the terrace. My feet didn't touch the ground for the next few minutes as we swayed from side to side and up and down. There were two reasons why it was difficult to catch your breath, the first was the intensity of the match, the second was because your ribs were crushed up against your lungs. I don't believe we stopped singing the whole game, the stadium was deafening. Then Bryan Robson scored and we had a chance. Then Frank Stapleton took a shot that the goalkeeper fumbled and Robson followed in to score again. Now we all believed. Come on United you can do it. Stapleton added a third with a volley and the most glorious night in twenty years was won. We had beaten the tournament favorites 3-2 on aggregate after losing the first leg 2-0. I couldn't speak for two days, my voice belonged to the football gods.

Bryan Robson said that the atmosphere at Old Trafford that night was the best he ever witnessed as a player. He added that the pitch was shaking. The Stretford End certainly was, and so was I.

Injuries and a good Juventus side knocked us out at the semi final stage. Robson, Wilkins and Muhren all missed the games and without our talisman, Juventus were too good. But nobody can ever forget the game against Barcelona. Now every rich club in the world wanted to sign Bryan Robson. Bryan wanted to stay at Manchester United. Despite a season with no trophies, the horizon was very bright.

Big Norm and Kevin Moran for PM

The FA Cup provided the only taste of glory for Big Ron, but we had our moments of hope in the league. In 1995 we had two Merseyside giants to contend with as a resurgent Everton, under Howard Kendall, were sweeping all before them. United once again finished the league campaign in fourth place after flattering to deceive for most of the season.

I missed the cup semi final against Liverpool at Maine Road as I was away. The game ended in a draw and so it was back to Goodison Park, Everton's home, for the replay. Again I missed the game but caught it on the radio as I raced back to Manchester from the South of England.

Ray Wilkins had been sold to AC Milan and Remi Moses had been injured, hampering his expected progress into the first team. Norman Whiteside was now playing in midfield and a youngster called Mark Hughes was the new darling of the Stretford End. Bryan Robson was still the main man, having become captain of both United and England and being nicknamed by the press as Captain Marvel. Liverpool were losing out to Everton in the league title race and were determined to get to the FA Cup final to continue their run of trophies. We had other ideas of course.

As I drove home I could sense the atmosphere through the radio speakers. All I could hear were United songs, repeated over and over again. The commentators were less biased in those days and actually talked about what was happening on the pitch, rather than spouting off their claptrap like they do today in a vain attempt to sound intelligent.

Liverpool took an early lead and I feared the worst. Then, as I thought I was listening to the description of another scouse attack, I heard "Robson, he's found space, what a goal by Bryan Robson." He had broken up the Liverpool attack, played a one two with Whiteside and then blasted a magnificent left foot shot past the helpless Grobbelar. A few minutes later and again the commentators created mayhem, until I heard through the excitement that Mark Hughes had surely put us through to the FA Cup Final. I was screaming at the top of my voice before looking at the speedometer on the hire car. Wow Bobby, a hundred and ten might attract a bit of attention. I slowed down to eighty, still screaming. I couldn't wait to see the highlights that night and boy were they worth watching. The Robson and Hughes goals were even better than the radio commentators had described.

The final was another momentous occasion. It was also when I really started to get angry at how pathetic the allocation of tickets to each club was made. There were more hangers on than real fans and the teams didn't get an allocation anything like their home attendances. How could a real fan ever get to see his or her team at Wembley?

I watched the game at Graham Banks-Popples' house. A friend I met when I joined British Aerospace and who had become a regular with us at Old Trafford. James, my nearly two year old toddler, came with me, enjoying his first FA Cup Final.

The game was cagey and Everton were seeking a league and FA Cup double for the first time in their history. There were few chances at either end when Kevin Moran was adjudged to have fouled Peter Reid, the Everton midfield player. Although the foul occurred at the half way line, Reid was never going to get close to the United goal, and that Moran actually got some of the ball, the referee sent him off. We were down to ten men against the best team in the country that year. Where was that referee two years earlier when Grobbelar committed GBH on Gordon McQueen? The game went into extra time and the United players were visibly tiring. Hughes was playing more in midfield than attack when he received the ball on the half way line, he turned inside an Everton defender and played an inch perfect pass to Norman Whiteside in the outside right position. Norman, gave a quick stepover to find space and curled a beauty, past Neville Southall into the far corner of the goal. The Banks-Popple house shuddered as Graham and I leapt to our feet screaming and jumping before I remembered James was there and had to re-assure him that everything was okay. I taught him his first United song on the way home that afternoon and he's been as addicted as me ever since.

Norman has been a legend ever since that glorious goal, two years after he had become the youngest ever scorer in an FA Cup Final.

At the traditional homecoming, the United players appeared on the balcony at the town hall in Albert Square. Kevin Moran was seen yelling to the crowd about how magnificent they were. The crowd of course obligingly screamed back. It was the start of a tremendous love affair between the United faithful and the brave Irishman. A defender that I've seen stretchered off the field with blood pouring from a head wound on so many occasions that I can't count them. For Kevin, his passionate speech to the Albert Square crowd, prompted some to suggest he become a politician after retiring from the game. Fortunately that hasn't yet happened.

Later that summer, my second child Jennifer was born, twenty two months after James. A joyous occasion but it put unbearable financial burden on me. Unfortunately my car also broke down due to lack of maintenance. This was the third time I had lost a car because I couldn't afford to maintain it. I had to cycle to work for a year or so, in all conditions. I also had to work as much overtime as I could get but at least I still had United and two wonderful kids.

Sports Report and Why You Should Never Leave Early

Before the advent of Satellite TV and the internet we got most of our live information about football from the radio. Television wasn't yet ruling football and almost without exception, all games kicked off at three o'clock on a Saturday afternoon.

The Scoreboard at Old Trafford was state of the art at the time because it flashed up the half time scores from around the country on an electric scoreboard. However, you needed to know how to navigate the system because the scoreboard would say A 1-0, B 0-1 etc. The match day programme listed which games were A, B, C. We were always ready to cheer at the misfortune of our rivals.

At the end of the game we would rush back to the car and switch on the Radio. At five o'clock on radio five there was a programme called sports report where we would officially find out how well, or otherwise, our rivals had done. When all the results had been reported, they would get a report from all the top games. Often the reporter from Old Trafford would have seen a different game to the one we had watched. The sports report show was a welcome sidetrack to the horrendous traffic jams we had to endure on the way home. Avoiding these jams is probably why some people leave the ground before the final whistle.

I've never understood leaving early, especially if you are a United fan. Over the years there have been many last minute goals and why pay for a hard earned ticket and not see the whole game? I remember one game, at home to Oxford United. I can't remember which season but it was one of the twenty six that we didn't win the league. At half time United were cruising 2-0. In the second half we didn't play. Oxford scored two goals and as the game approached the last two minutes it looked like we were heading for another disappointing draw. Chris and Ste had had enough and left the ground. This was doubly surprising because I was driving and they couldn't get home anyway. Up stepped Bryan Robson with a winning goal that was pretty much the last kick of the game. Julian, Mick and I had great pleasure glowing about it being the best goal ever until sports report called it a scramble. Who cares? We had won in the last minute and I've never left a game early in my life.

When The Skinflints Cost Us The League

United had been generous with the cash for Big Ron and we were all expecting the same at the start of the 1985/86 season. The lads and I felt we needed to strengthen in three areas. Gary Bailey had suffered a couple of injuries and was now unsure of his place in the first team. The other goalkeeper, Chris Turner was an outstanding talent but too small. He was a great shot stopper but a little fragile in the air. Everton had won the league the previous season largely because they had Neville Southall, in our opinion the best goalkeeper in the world. Southall wasn't available but Peter Shilton, the England goalkeeper could surely have been prized from Nottingham Forest.

In central defence both Martin Buchan and Gordon McQueen had gone. A rookie called Paul McGrath had stepped up and looked very useful. McGrath was a tremendous athlete and very skilled but still untried. Kevin Moran was a hero and very brave but that bravery meant he was often injured. The other alternative was Graeme Hogg. Hoggy was competent in the air and a real battler but was he good enough? We felt we needed experience and who better than Terry Butcher, the England centre half. Butch was available as well and expressed a desire to join us from Ipswich.

The final piece of the jigsaw would have been to find a strike partner for Mark Hughes. Frank Stapleton was a good player but he didn't score enough goals. Gary Lineker was leaving Leicester City and he scored goals for fun.

Our first eleven was as good as anybody and our midfield was by far the best in the league, with the peerless Bryan Robson ably supported by the always improving Norman Whiteside. On the flanks we had wee Gordon Strachan and Jesper Olsen, the nineteen eighties version of Coppell and Hill. The problem was strength in depth. A couple of injuries and we struggled.

As the season approached, it became obvious we weren't going to spend any real money. Shilton stayed at Forest, Butcher joined Rangers, presumably to play the European football that was now denied to English clubs following the disaster at Heysel. Lineker joined Everton with United suggesting they felt a Hughes Lineker partnership wouldn't work.

For a while it seemed to work out. United won their first ten games of the new season, leaping into a ten point lead. One of those games was away to Chelsea at Stamford Bridge. We won 2-1 with a screamer from Hughes sealing the victory after we played most of the second half with ten men. We also beat City at Maine Road in the Manchester derby. At the end of those games we'd scored twenty six and conceded just three.

Then the wheels started to fall off. We scraped a draw against QPR. Injuries meant we never knew who would be playing in defence, or midfield; and the goals dried up. Even Frank Stapleton was playing some of the games as a centre half. Bryan Robson had dislocated his shoulder and seemed to re-injure it at every attempted comeback. We were still in contention in March but it was looking bleak. The wags on United Road had seen it all before and there was a reservation when we played Chelsea in a night match at Old Trafford. A win would have taken us back to the top of the league. Kerry Dixon, the Chelsea striker had other ideas and we slumped to a 2-1 defeat with Dixon out-sprinting our tired defenders to score both goals for Chelsea.

Key injuries had hurt the team, lack of quality cover had hurt the team, but the root cause was not investing in the right players when they had been available the previous summer.

To make matters worse, Lineker had scored a bagful for Everton but Liverpool won their last twelve games to become champions again. Those buggers from Merseyside were really getting on my nerves now.

The Second Dynasty

The following season started as badly as the previous one ended. Bryan Robson aggravated the shoulder injury at the World Cup with England and missed the first four games. We lost three of them.

The board reacted to the fierce and justified criticism of their transfer policy by buying anybody who played well against us. This included Colin Gibson who arrived mid season the previous year from Aston Villa, Terry Gibson, a striker from Wimbledon who made Ronnie Corbett look tall, and Peter Davenport from Nottingham Forest. We also sold Mark Hughes to Barcelona, who also bought Gary Lineker from Everton. They obviously didn't consult the United board for an opinion about the likely success of a Hughes Lineker partnership.

The only minor success of these new buys was Colin Gibson who could play left midfield or left full back if and when Arthur Albiston was unavailable. Colin had a neat step over move that freed space to make crosses into the opposition penalty area. The trouble is that most of his crosses ended up in row Z of K stand, causing the United Road crowd to shout duck every time he shaped up to cross the ball.

Terry Gibson scored one goal in dozens of matches and Peter Davenport fared little better. He had looked good at Forest but was a lightweight and not suited to our style of play that required the main striker to hold the ball up for oncoming midfield players.

Davenport was the third player we had bought from Nottingham Forest during my time as a fan. All of them had been total failures. Storey Moore failed through injury that was no fault of his own. Birtles and Davenport failed because they either didn't have the ability, or they couldn't cope with the pressure of playing for the biggest club in the world. Forest must have seen us coming.

The crowds were now shrinking as well. It was almost twenty years since the last league title and the team was not getting any closer to winning it again. In November 1986, Big Ron was fired.

United turned once again to Scotland and persuaded Alex Ferguson to leave Aberdeen to take the hot seat at United. Fergie had been a phenomenon at Aberdeen, breaking the old firm stranglehold on trophies and even winning the European Cup Winners Cup against all the odds. Could he do the same at United? I was standing on the Stretford End the day he was introduced to the faithful. If he didn't know the magnitude of the task facing him he soon would. His first game in charge was away to Oxford United at the Manor Ground. United were poor and lost 2-0. The team was in disarray, the fans restless and the title a million miles away. The new boss could only take us in one direction.

Fergie didn't make wholesale changes immediately. He had no choice. The youth structure, one of the great successes over the years wasn't producing. The only player in the reserves with any potential was Nicky Wood, a fast skilful forward who would surely have made an impact had he not suffered a recurring back injury. One of the first tasks was to rebuild the youth system to get the pipeline of future stars coming through.

We had a few highlights in Fergie's first six months in charge like a league double over both City and Liverpool before finishing in eleventh place.

Fergie got busy in his first close season in charge, bringing in Brian McLair from Celtic to replace Frank Stapleton who was sold to Ajax. Ferguson had been an admirer of McLair during his time at Aberdeen. He also brought in Viv Anderson from Arsenal and he immediately helped to strengthen the defence. United finished the season really strongly, remaining unbeaten in the league for the last three months of the season. The highlight for the United fans was in delaying Liverpool's inevitable charge to yet another title with a thrilling three all draw at Anfield. Bryan Robson had given us the lead but when Colin Gibson was dismissed, Liverpool scored three times. At 3-1 down and a man short, it looked hopeless. But a typical second goal from Bryan Robson, who never gave up and an equalizer from Gordon Strachan in front of a disbelieving Kop gave us a share of the points.

In the next close season, Fergie brought in his old Aberdeen goalkeeper, Jim Leighton. He also brought Mark Hughes back after indifferent spells with Barcelona and Bayern Munich. He also let some of the older stars leave including Arthur Albiston and Kevin Moran.

A young Lee Sharpe was bought from Torquay United and he excelled at either left back or left wing. Other youngsters coming through included Russell Beardsmore, a crafty midfield player, and Lee Martin a really solid looking full back. Another youth player who made an impact was striker Mark Robins. The first task of re-invigorating the youth system was starting to pay off. The season didn't start too well though and in the autumn of 1988, United didn't win in nine games. They did, however, buy a promising centre half from Norwich City and the legend that is Steve Bruce made an immediate impact at the heart of the defence. As usual though, his arrival coincided with the start of a series of injuries to Paul McGrath, delaying the start of what was hoped to be an unbeatable partnership.

My autumn in 1988 was a lot better. I had been promoted, was driving a newish car and was present at the birth of Charlotte my third child.

I had also joined Bolton Health studio and often shared a beer with Alan Gowling after a workout. Alan was a former United star who was now chairman of their old boys. He told me to be patient and quietly confident as United were going in the right direction both on and off the field. Now if only United could back up Alan's optimism.

The lads in Little Lever had a pretty good routine by now. We would meet in the Jolly Carters pub for a quick beer before travelling to Old Trafford some ten miles away. After the game we would drive back, the driver would deposit his car at home, we'd all have a quick bite to eat and then meet back at the Jolly's to discuss the game – again! In 1988, this was usually about why we had once again failed to hold on to a lead against inferior opposition.

We needed some Christmas cheer and looked forward to a couple of home games against Nottingham Forest and Liverpool. We had also made the most baffling signing of my entire life in supporting United. Ralph Milne, who nobody had ever heard of arrived from one of the Bristol clubs. On Boxing Day we beat Forest 2-0 with Ralphie scoring the first goal – amazing. Following a typically raucous and wild New Years Eve, the gang from Little Lever made our way wearily to Old Trafford for the New Years Day clash with Liverpool. I gave in to peer pressure and joined my mates again on the Stretford End. We absolutely battered Liverpool for seventy minutes but didn't manage to break the deadlock. Liverpool winger John Barnes then got on the end of a breakaway and scored. Surely we couldn't play this well and not win. Never fear, the newly christened Fergie Fledglings did us proud and within seven minutes of mayhem in front of a mad Stretford End, we were 3-1 up. I remember young Beardsmore scoring the third from a Lee Sharpe cross but can't remember who scored the other two. I remember a similar experience to the one I witnessed on the night against Barcelona when my feet didn't touch the ground for five minutes as I swayed up and down and left and right across the area close to the tunnel. Standing on the terraces at football matches was the greatest experience anybody could witness.

That winter I played a friendly match at The Cliff, Manchester United's training ground in Salford. A group of us from British Aerospace took on the United Stewards. One of the stewards looked familiar. He was Deniol Graham who was just breaking through to the United first team. He had scored in a cup game against QPR that season and there I was playing against him. He was recovering from a broken arm and playing in a protective cast. I'm sure Fergie didn't know, or maybe that's why Deniol only played three times for the first team! Playing on a full sized indoor field was great. Knowing that earlier that day the United squad had trained there was even better.

Nineteen eighty nine started on a real high but our league form let us down and we stumbled to another eleventh place finish. We could and perhaps should have won the FA Cup that year. We played Nottingham

Forest at home in the quarter final, buoyed by the slaughtering we gave them on Boxing Day. In a good game that we dominated, Forest took the lead against the run of play. Shortly afterwards Brian McLair scored the equalizer in front of a jumping and screaming Stretford End. But just like the Dennis Law goal against Milan some twenty years earlier, Mr. Magoos' son, alias Brian Hill, failed to see the ball cross the line, even though TV replays showed it was at least two feet over. We were out and Forest went on to play Liverpool at Hillsborough.

What happened next was one of the worse tragedies in football, with 96 Liverpool fans losing their lives. But for the grace of God and a different referee in the quarter finals it could have been us. On the day of the semi final we played Derby County in a nothing game at Old Trafford. The Stretford End was only about eighty per cent full as we contemplated another season of near misses. Half way through the first half the stadium announcer advised that crowd trouble at Hillsborough had delayed the start. All the usual scouse jokes started, along with a few songs. A few minutes later the announcer came on again, telling us that the game at Hillsborough had been abandoned and that many people had lost their lives. Our jokes turned to silence. If anybody denies the deep horror we felt that day on the Stretford End as the game petered out to a 2-0 home defeat, they are lying. The tragic loss of lives amongst the supporters of our bitter rivals was just as shocking for those of us at the Manchester end of the East Lancashire Road.

Michael Knighton, Robert Maxwell and Rupert Murdock

It was at the start of the 1989/90 season that a previously unheard of Michael Knighton appeared on the scene. Knighton had apparently bought the majority shareholding of the club from Martin Edwards. This was a surprise because Robert Maxwell had tried to do the same a few years earlier, only to be totally re-buffed. This was despite promising to buy Maradona and Zico for us once he took over.

The news of the Knighton takeover appeared in the papers on the Saturday morning before the first home game against reigning champions Arsenal. As we prepared for the game, again on the Stretford End, a rather chubby man wearing a United track suit top ran on to the field juggling a ball between both his feet before firing the ball into the goal immediately below us. It was Michael Knighton, the new chairman.

In the close season Fergie brought in Neil Webb, the England midfield maestro from Nottingham Forest and Mike Phelan from Norwich. Any concerns I had about buying another player from Forest were quickly dispersed as Webby dominated the game, scoring a fine volley in a 4-1 win against the reigning champions.

My son James was now six years old and enjoying his football. I would occasionally take him to games and he remembers early days when he would sit on a barrier at the front of the Stretford End. Jennifer's first game was still a few years away. Our big concern was Charlotte. All three kids had been fed on Soya milk following a recommendation by the midwife to avoid a repeat of my eczema and their mothers' asthma. Unfortunately,

Charlotte was allergic to soya and as a consequence was not putting any weight on. It was a massive relief when we discovered the problem and she started to gain weight as normal.

The opening game against Arsenal was to be my last that season. British Aerospace was closing down the office in Bolton and I was offered a promotion if I moved to Stevenage.

A few days before we moved, the Forest curse struck again. Neil Webb tore his cruciate ligament while playing for England. Although he did return later that season, he was never the same player. I believe he is now a postman.

Shortly after the season started we also recruited Gary Pallister to partner Steve Bruce. Pally was a then record signing for a centre half when we persuaded Middlesborough to let him join us. Paul Ince was also recruited from West Ham with an eye for the future and Danny Wallace from Southampton to give us an extra dimension of pace and trickery on the wing. Gordon Strachan was controversially sold to Leeds, the second time in his career that Fergie had let him go.

Inevitably the Michael Knighton takeover was nothing more than a charade as he didn't have the finances to take over the club. He was offered a position on the board which he maintained for a short period. The off-field farce hardly helped the team to settle. It did, however, shore up the clubs management structure. One of the reasons the takeover had been accepted was to inject funds for the redevelopment of the Stretford End. When the takeover collapsed, the projected funds disappeared too. United had no choice but to go public and we were floated on the stock exchange. Going public enabled ordinary supporters to own shares in the club they loved. This paid dividends a few years later as fans were able to stop an attempted takeover by Rupert Murdoch, the owner of Sky television. The David and Goliath victory was masterminded by an organization called Shareholders United who have since become the Manchester United Supporters Trust.

Moving To Cambridge and a New Kind of Banter

Although I was now working in Stevenage, we lived in Cambridgeshire in a lovely village called Great Paxton. There was one pub, The Bell, otherwise known as village HQ, a tenth century church, a small shop cum post office and a junior school. There was also a recreation ground where Great Paxton Football Club played their home games.

The move initially went very smoothly, with British Aerospace providing much needed assistance. That was until our house in Little Lever was sold for eight thousand pounds less than the minimum price we had told the agent we would accept. This was the second time that I had been ripped off by incompetent so called British professionals. I wish I could remember the name of the agent because I would love to shame him and his boss, but it was almost twenty years ago. What happened was the Black Horse agency, who had been employed by British Aerospace to facilitate the move and house sale, had accepted an offer without consulting with us. When I challenged them they said it was in everybody's interest to accept a quick sale and as I hadn't responded to their request for acceptance, they applied the conditions in the small print and sold the property. The truth is that these idiots hadn't tried to contact me at all. The agent had the bloody cheek to ask how my holiday in the South of France had gone, suggesting that was the reason I had failed to get back to them within the stipulated timescale. What a nerve. I hadn't been to the South of France since 1976. I can't tell you how angry I was with Black Horse, their staff, their lack of moral fibre and their sheer incompetence. It set us back a number of years in completing our planned house improvements.

The Bell pub was my refuge from the Black Horse fiasco and I soon got in with the local crowd. It was strange though because for the first time in my life I was mixing with football fans that didn't all support United. Tony was a Spurs fan, Ray supported Millwall, Clive liked West Ham and Martin was a QPR fan. There were others as well. Needless to say, the banter was a bit different.

Soon after moving into Great Paxton, I was talking with Tony and Ray when Martin joined us. It was a Friday evening and Martin was drinking coke because he was playing for the Paxton team the following day. The subject got around to my playing days and Martin suggested that I watch the team the following day where he would introduce me to Sean Maloney, the team manager. Martin was obviously impressed by the fact I'd played in the Lancashire and Cheshire league and less bothered that I hadn't played for several years.

I was pleasantly surprised by the standard and was persuaded to sign on for the team, maybe even getting a ten minute run out the following Saturday. The following day I flew to Washington DC for the first time, returning on Thursday morning after an overnight flight that left me jet lagged and exhausted. I was shocked on Friday when Sean phoned to say that the usual striker was injured and that I would be starting the next day. They had never seen me play and I was totally out of condition. It was a disaster waiting to happen.

The game flew by me and I was substituted mid way through the second half. I could barely walk for two days but the love of playing was back and I played for Great Paxton until I moved to Washington DC in 1995.

Meanwhile, the Red Devils failed to capitalize on the win against Arsenal and were stuttering again in the league. They hadn't won a trophy since the FA Cup victory in 1985 and there were rumours of Ferguson being replaced. More games were being televised now, especially in the FA Cup where for the second season running United were playing Nottingham Forest, this time at the City Ground. It has been said many times that if United had lost, it would have been the end of Fergie, although it has also been denied that this was the case. United had a new look, a new style that blended solid defending with flair and attractive attacking football. Kids were given a chance and the youth set up was encouraging. The problem as always was injuries. The dream team midfield of Robson, Webb and Phelan never got going with Robson and Webb out for most of the season. Whiteside had been shipped off to Everton.

Fortunately, the board didn't have to make a decision on Fergusons future because a Mark Robins goal helped United secure a 1-0 win and exact revenge on Forest for the defeat the previous year. Progress through the FA Cup brought some joy to the fans and we eagerly awaited the semi final. That year, both games were televised and played on the same day. Crystal Palace beat Liverpool in a remarkable game that finished 4-3. The United versus Oldham game had a lot to live up to. However, live up to it they did. In front of a capacity crowd at Maine Road, the teams fought out a 3-3 draw. United won the replay 2-1 with Mark Robins again the hero, scoring the winner. United would face Crystal Palace in the final.

Super Lee Martin

I tried but failed to get a ticket for the Cup Final which as usual were like gold dust. All the lads from Little Lever made it though and had great fun calling me on match day to tell me they were just about to get on the coach.

I settled in front of the TV in the living room with a couple of beers and an expectant son who was now as keen as I was. It was another typical United game, ebbing and flowing one way then the other. It finally ended up 3-3 with Mark Hughes grabbing two goals for United and Palace substitute Ian Wright grabbing a couple for the Eagles. The replay was set for the following Thursday.

Imagine my surprise the next day when Ste Howarth called and said he could get me a ticket if I wanted one. If I wanted one! What sort of a question was that. I graciously accepted, screamed so loud that I scared the kids and headed straight to the Bell for a celebration pint or two. Returning later to teach the kids how to sing "Wemberley, Wemberley, we're the famous Man United and we're going to Wemberley." Charlotte was still singing it a few months later.

The big day finally arrived and I left work early to head to the meeting point outside Stanmore tube station. The area was flooded with reds and I was a bit concerned that I might have missed Ste, Mick, Julian and Ste's younger brother Paul. The hour that I was standing at the entrance to the station seemed like a lifetime as thousands of reds and an occasional Palace fan filtered by. Crystal Palace is based South of the Thames and most of their fans live in that area, hence the relatively low number catching the tube at its Northern most point.

Eventually the lads arrived and I exchanged my hard earned cash for the ticket.

The tube journey was fantastic. We were packed in like sardines and sang all the way to the Wembley tube station. All the great old songs were performed and repeated. Favorites like; 'She wore a scarlet ribbon', 'Ce cera cera', and 'Pride of all Europe.' The walk down Wembley way towards the twin towers was equally exciting.

This was my first visit to Wembley since 1985 when for my sins I attended a Bruce Springsteen concert, and I had forgotten what an absolute dump the place was. Never mind, I wasn't there to admire the scenery, I was there to watch United.

Once inside the ground, the first thing I noticed was how three quarters of the stadium was decked out in red and white. Replays were less likely to be sold out to corporate sponsors and hangers on and so real fans had more chance of getting a ticket. The second thing I noticed was the noise. The United fans were in tremendous voice. Then a shock! Jim Leighton, the United keeper had been dropped, allegedly and correctly in my opinion he had been blamed for two of the Palace goals in the first game and his confidence was shattered. I don't remember Leighton ever playing for us again. Replacing him in goal was Les Sealey, a journeyman keeper who had recently arrived as cover. Sealey was actually a good keeper and very brave, just what the doctor ordered.

I had a great seat above the tunnel behind one of the goals. Neil Webb was back, although clearly not fully fit, and Robson and Ince were there too. The game was not exactly a classic and Palace used some rough tactics to try to unsettle Sealey. These tactics were a bit of a surprise as their manager was none other than our own Steve Coppell. Half time arrived without too much incident, United dominating possession but Palace having their moments as well. The second half was almost all United but Palace were hanging on. As the game went on, Neil Webb became more involved and he played a superb chipped through ball to Lee Martin, the left back who must have got a nose bleed being that far forward. Lee instantly had the ball under control, chesting it and then half volleying it in one graceful move. We held our breath and then jumped and screamed as we saw the net bulge. We had won the FA Cup again and Ferguson had his first trophy as United manager.

All the way home we sang "Who put the ball in the Palace net? – Super Lee Martin."

Rotterdam

Everybody expected United to be going places now, and they didn't disappoint. Lee Sharpe was improving all the time and many of the older players were in their prime. The central defensive partnership of Steve Bruce and Gary Pallister was as good as United had seen in thirty years. Now all we had to do was keep Bryan Robson fit and surely we would win the league.

The other good news was that English teams were once again allowed in Europe following the five year ban given in the aftermath of the Heysel disaster.

Great Paxton were playing well and I had a new strike partner in Ian Gabriel. Gabby, as he was known, was as quick as lightening and my vision and passing complemented his style. The only fault Gabby had was his love for Arsenal. One of our players, Clive Edwards had a long term injury and he would always stand on the touchline with a transistor radio in his hand. He took great joy in shouting out the United scores to me. He later told me that he sometimes made them up depending on how I was playing. He said that when he told me that United had scored, it would inspire me to try defence splitting passes and control the game. When he told me we'd conceded a goal, it made me angry and more aggressive. Thanks Clive.

United started in Europe the way they meant to go on, with a 3-0 aggregate victory against Pecsi Munkas of Hungary (or Pesky Monkeys as we called them). We then strolled by Wrexham, the Welsh Cup Winners 5-0, putting us into a quarter final that would have to wait until March the following year. The League Cup, now called the Rumbellows Cup after the high street firm that were now its' principal sponsors, was also providing some memorable moments. A 3-1 win over Liverpool in the 3rd round was greeted with the usual ecstasy but it was the 5th round that provided the best moment of the competition. We were drawn away to Arsenal, the defending league champions and Gabby was very confident that his boys would turn us over. I threatened to stop passing to him if they did. The game was amazing. United were 3-0 up at half time. Then Arsenal scored two quick goals at the beginning of the second half and we feared the worst. Our fears were unfounded though as United scored three more to win 6-2 at Highbury. United were most definitely back. Our league form was a big improvement on recent years but all the cup distractions meant that we had to eventually settle for sixth place. Forcing a still shell-shocked Gabby to advise me that United might be a good bet for a cup, but they'd never win the league. Well mate, we shall see about that.

Back in Europe we beat Montpelier of France 3-1 in the quarter finals, setting up a hectic end to an exciting season. We then had two, two legged semi finals, one against Leeds in the Rumbellows Cup, the other against Legia Warsaw in the European Cup Winners Cup. After two tough but successful games against Leeds we travelled to Warsaw and ran out 3-1 winners. The second leg would have to wait until after the Rumbellows Cup Final against another Yorkshire team, Sheffield Wednesday.

On paper, we should have beaten Wednesday easily. The four Wednesday fans that lived in Paxton and frequented the Bell thought so too. Football is not, has not and never will be played on paper and Wednesday scored a surprising 1-0 victory. We had two choices, mope around in disappointment or focus on the European semi final. Thankfully we did the latter and a Lee Sharpe goal gave us a 1-0 win and a 4-1 aggregate victory. Now all we had to do was beat Barcelona again in Rotterdam, in the final.

I was back in the North West on the 15th May 1991 and rather than watch the game in my hotel room, I called Ste to invite myself over to his house. He graciously picked me up at the Georgian Hotel in Horwich and I joined Ste and Paul and all the other lads who used to watch the games with me, Mick, Chris and Julian. Clive Edwards in Paxton to this day believes it was all a front and that I was really in Rotterdam and I wish that was the case, but I really did watch the game in Ste Howarth's living room in Little Lever. And what a game! United's amazing flying team against Barcelona's all star cast. An early chance fell to Brian McLair who was through, one on one with the Barcelona keeper. Just as he was about to shoot the ball bobbled to shin height and he spooned it high, wide and not very handsome. Ste's Dad couldn't watch any more, claiming that by missing that chance we would eventually succumb to the mighty Spaniards. Oh yea of little faith. Mid way through the second half, Bryan Robson chipped an exquisite free kick into the Barcelona penalty area. Steve Bruce powerfully met the ball with his head and Mark Hughes followed up, crashing the ball into the empty net. There have been arguments about who scored that goal but come on – who cares – it was 1-0 to United. The Howarth's bungalow was bouncing. A few minutes later and Mark Hughes ran on to a pinpoint through pass and flicked the ball past the keeper. We held our breath as we thought he'd been forced too far wide to the right but Hughes had other ideas and smacked a scorcher past a despairing Barcelona defender. A late Ronald Koeman trademark free kick was nothing more than a consolation for the Spanish giants and United were once again champions of Europe. I believe that the Howarth's neighbours put their house on the market the following day. We sang our hearts out as we walked across the road to the Jolly Carter's and then drank ourselves silly until closing time. I can't remember how much the taxi back to the Georgian House cost me; and I didn't care.

We had developed a nice habit of winning important trophies and being competitive in every game. Surely we were now ready to make a real assault on the league championship. Even Fergie was bold enough to suggest so.

Another Reason To Hate Leeds

Fergie strengthened the team again in the close season, bringing in the great Danish goalkeeper, Peter Schmeichel. A young Welsh boy named Ryan Giggs had also made his way into the team from the all conquering youth team. He also brought in a flying Ukranian called Andrei Kanchelskis who made Lee Sharpe look slow.

My job was taking me all over Europe now and one of the perks of flying business class on British Airways was the quarter sized bottles of Champagne. I would often smooth talk the flight attendants to let me take a couple home with me and made quite a stash, ready to be unleashed and uncorked when we won the league.

The first game of the new season was at home to Notts County. Getting a ticket for James and I was a priority and at the suggestion of Chris Beavan, another United fan who lived in the village, we joined the Manchester United Official Supporters Club, East Anglia Branch. The supporters club would not only get tickets but also provide a seat on the official coach to and from Old Trafford. This was alas going to be the last season that terracing would be allowed in the top flight of English football and I had to witness the Stretford End again. United Road had already gone with seats replacing the once proud terrace. They even renamed it the North Stand but to real fans it will always be called United Road.

James, Chris and I caught the coach in Godmanchester, the closest stop to Great Paxton and made our way to the game. When the teams came out to warm up we couldn't believe the size of Schmeichel.

He was a colossus with massive hands and great reflexes. United won the game 2-0 and the new season was off to the right start.

In Europe, an early exit from the European Cup Winners Cup at the hands of Atletico Madrid was offset by victory against Red Star Belgrade in the European Super Cup. Brian McClair scored the only goal of a competitive game against the European Cup holders.

The first half of the domestic season was great with United playing uninhibited free flowing football that was the envy of everybody. At the beginning of 1992 we had to play our closest rivals, Leeds, three times in two weeks, all at Elland Road. United dominated the mini-series, knocking the Yorkshire club out of the FA Cup, 1-0; the Rumbellows Cup, 3-1; and only a last gasp penalty for the home side cost us a whitewash, the league game ending 1-1. In retrospect, that mini-series may have cost us the title because it freed Leeds to concentrate on the league.

The Rumbellows Cup provided our second trophy of the season as we beat Nottingham Forest in the final; again Brian McLair scored the only goal of a good game.

The downside to all the cup success was a congested fixture list and United had to play their last six league games in seventeen days. The fixtures came thick and fast and we lost three of those games. At Elland Road, a certain Frenchman called Eric Cantona had found his scoring touch and helped Leeds claim the title.

Even Howard Wilkinson, the triumphant Leeds manager at the time, admitted that United had been dealt a cruel blow having to play all those games in such a little time.

That summer was dreadful and the champagne had to stay on ice for another year at least.

Twenty Six Bloody Years

It was now twenty five years since the last title in 1967. By the end of the 1992/93 season it would be twenty six years. In that time we had been close but never quite made it, coming second on four occasions and third on three occasions. During that time our three biggest rivals, Arsenal, Liverpool and Leeds had won the title on multiple occasions. Even teams like Nottingham Forest and Aston Villa had lifted the first division title. The biggest insult though was that Manchester City had been crowned the champions of England since we had.

Manchester United must be jinxed I thought and wondered if the devil nickname had something to do with it. I even sent a letter to Old Trafford on one occasion suggesting that we change the nickname to the Red Angels to see if we could get God back on our side.

The Football Association, another group who I'd lost faith with, had decided to change the top flight of English football. It was gradually reduced from 22 teams to 20, enabling four fewer games each season in an attempt to help England be more competitive. At Old Trafford we were sick of England because it seemed that every time we had a star player in the England team, we would lose them to a serious injury. Bryan Robson, Ray Wilkins and Neil Webb were cases in point. At the end of the day, the FA's intention was all about marketing and the new league was to be called the Premier League.

We started the Premier League as clear favorites but early defeats, including a 3-0 thrashing at home to Everton, soon had the bookies changing their minds.

August and September offered little suggestion that the wait would be over and I was glad to be playing for Great Paxton on Saturdays. With the exception of a home game against Wimbledon, another 1-0 defeat, I missed the United season, settling for TV highlights.

I remember the day it all changed very clearly. I was driving home from work when the news came on the radio. Eric Cantona had been signed by Fergie for a ridiculously low price of one million pounds. I sang 'Ooh Aah Cantona' all the way home. Leeds might as well have handed over the trophy at the same time but there was still a lot of work to do.

Cantona settled in immediately and scored in four of his first six games. The Red Devils were climbing up the table. Our nearest rivals that year were Aston Villa and Norwich. It seemed like the other top flight teams were taking it in turns to try and deny United the title.

There was to be one more massive turning point that season. I was on holiday with the family in Brixham, Devon. The Wall Park Pontins Holiday Centre had been our Easter destination for a number of years. We met the same families every year for a week of health, fitness, football, volleyball, entertainment and of course, beer drinking.

United had enjoyed some excellent victories away at Anfield and at Norwich, against a surprising but worthy East Anglian title contender. All we had to do was win our remaining fixtures and we would be champions. Only Aston Villa could stop us and an exciting 1-1 draw at Old Trafford just before Easter kept the title wide open.

With just a few games left, I huddled up to listen to the radio in the Pontins chalet. We were playing Sheffield Wednesday at Old Trafford in a game we were expected to win. United dominated possession but on 64 minutes Wednesday broke downfield. Chris Waddle ran into the penalty area and was tripped. The referee had no option but to award a spot kick and an old nemesis called John Sheridan put the visitors one nil ahead. It was the referees first decision of the game because shortly beforehand, the original referee fell awkwardly and injured himself. It took about eight minutes before the game re-started and we all prayed that the replacement had a good watch. There is an amazing vision of a United supporter in tears behind the Scoreboard End goal. He was so distraught that he staggered to his feet and left, convinced that we would blow the title again. The picture of this distressed fan has been seen by millions on various videos and DVDs and I still get a tear when I see him leave the stadium. With four minutes to go, we won a corner and Steve Bruce headed in a marvelous equalizer. There was still hope. With the clock ticking away, and six minutes of injury time played we forced another corner on the right. It was half cleared by the Wednesday defence but quickly retrieved just outside the box by Gary Pallister. His cross took a deflection and Steve Bruce somehow managed to get his head on the ball. What an amazing header by an amazing player. Our assistant manager, Brian Kidd, leapt for joy and jumped in the air on the pitch, shaking his fists wildly in delight towards the equally ecstatic crowd. I was going bananas in the chalet and anybody who knew me quickly guessed what had happened. The beer that night was sweeter than ever. I often wonder what happened to that distraught supporter and hope he heard the result soon enough to stop him jumping off the bridge into the Ship

Canal. I doubt he ever left a game before the final whistle again

On the last weekend of the season, Aston Villa played Oldham at Villa Park. Oldham was battling against relegation and so both sides had to win. Tears streamed down my face at the final whistle as Oldham beat Villa 1-0. The champagne was uncorked a few minutes later.

Twenty six bloody years of near misses, of false dawns and of broken dreams was over. Tears of pain had at last been traded for tears of joy. I wish I had been in Manchester that day for what by all accounts was the mother of all celebrations.

The First Double, Living In DC, and Meeting a Future Legend

Rather than rest on his laurels, Fergie looked to strengthen the squad. In the summer of 1993, he secured the signing of Irishman Roy Keane from Nottingham Forest for a UK record of three and three quarter million pounds. Needless to say, I was scared that we would soon be hearing of the end of Keane's career. I was also hoping that the Nottingham Forest curse only applied to English players.

I was travelling to the United States on a regular basis by now. Sometimes I'd be in Los Angeles and at other times it would be Washington DC. It put a real strain on my marriage but there were two important events that kept it together. I was adopting my fourth child, an amazing boy called Joe. Joe is special in that he was born with Downs Syndrome. The foster family he was living with were Spurs fans and consequently Joe spent the first eighteen months of his life supporting the wrong team. When at last he was ours, the first clothes I bought him included a United shirt. He has been okay ever since.

The other event surrounded my sister, Andrea, who was getting married in May 1994, on Cup Final day.

In January 1994, I flew into Heathrow from Washington DC. My usual routine was to take a quick shower in the British Airways Arrivals Lounge in Terminal Four, grab a quick breakfast, and go to work. There was a small TV in the breakfast bar area. The news took me completely by surprise. Matt Busby had died. The greatest manager the world had ever seen was no longer with us. I couldn't eat my breakfast and was so distraught that I went straight home, cancelling all the days' appointments.

United were amazing that season with Giggs and Kanchelskis flying down the wings and Eric pulling the strings. Keano settled in quickly and we won the league by a mile. I was in Los Angeles the day we beat Crystal Palace away to secure it but I managed to sneak out at lunchtime to a pub in Woodland Hills to watch the game. Needless to say I didn't return until the following morning.

We were also in the Cup Final. Andrea's wedding started on time at 2.00pm but she ignored my suggestion that we head quickly to the Novotel in Worsley for the photos. We did eventually get to the hotel just before half time and persuaded the hotel to set up a TV in the bar. Until it was in place I watched the final moments of the first half from the comfort of my hotel room. Half time arrived without any score and by all accounts Chelsea had the better chances. The second half was one of the most one sided displays of breathtaking football I ever remember seeing. We thumped them 4-0 and it could have been more. Our first ever double had been achieved.

Sir Matt Busby had seen our first title in twenty six years but didn't see the first double because he left this world in January of that year. He had also failed to see United re-live his dream by capturing the European Cup again. We would all have to wait a little while longer for that dream to come true.

At work, I was asked if I would take a secondment in Washington DC and accepted on condition that I could fly the kids across for the summer, and that I would be back in England at least once a month for meetings that

I could combine with family. For the first few weeks I stayed in the Ritz Carlton in Pentagon City. If you've never been in a Ritz, they are top class. The Front Desk Manager at the time was Jim Ryan, a terrific Irish lad from Cork. He was also a massive United fan. We immediately got along and often shared a beer or two in Ruby Tuesdays in the adjacent Pentagon City Mall. The major advantage of being friends with Jim was his uncanny ability to lose my reservation, only to recover the situation with an upgrade to a suite on the top floor. Jim and I watched many a game together in the bars around DC.

Nineteen Ninety Four was the year of the World Cup in America. A consultant I knew provided tickets for the World Cup group game between Norway and Mexico. I went to the RFK stadium, then home of the Washington Redskins American Football team. I was dressed in the Red United shirt of the day, the one with laces and a collar. The Mexican fans were amazing, making loads of noise despite having a terrible team. Hugo Sanchez of Real Madrid was their star man but he was past his prime. The only Norwegian player I recognized was their giant Spurs goalkeeper, Eric Thorsvedt.

Norway won the game 1-0 in the sweltering heat and humidity that is typical in June in DC. Getting back to the Ritz was a drag so I decided to have a beer in The Dubliner, just outside Union Station. That delay meant I arrived back at the Ritz just as a crowd of staff was gathering outside. Apparently the Norwegian team were staying there as well. We applauded them off the coach and I shouted well played to Eric who replied "Thanks, by the way, nice shirt." If you think that was cool what happened next was even better. Still wearing the shirt an hour or so later, I was in the hotel lift when two young men in blazers joined me. They were from the team and had name badges on. One of them was called Ronny Johnsen. I hadn't heard of either of them but they were really polite and Ronny said in a strong accent, "Manchester – Good team." This was two years before we signed him. If only I would have known!

Shortly afterwards I moved into an apartment on Crystal Drive in Crystal City. English football was difficult to find on American TV at the time and the internet hadn't really taken off. To keep up with United I had two choices, telephone the BBC and hope to get through to somebody who cared, or wait until the following day and buy the USA Today Newspaper where the scores could be found in the tiniest print on the last page of the sports page. I also joined the Gateway Health Club that was a short walk away. On Friday evenings the club had party time. Members could play volleyball and help themselves to a beer from the keg that was placed next to the court. Now that's what I call a health club.

The constant travel prior to moving to DC had placed an impossible strain on my marriage, that and the fact that I didn't look like Patrick Swayze; and I was now divorced. It didn't stop me visiting and having the kids as often as possible and they soon came across to see what all the fuss was about, staying for about four weeks.

This was the season that saw Eric Cantona's famous altercation with a Crystal Palace supporter that led to a nine month ban. That wasn't the first time the FA have done United an injustice and it wouldn't be the last. On the field, United were still formidable and with the added goal threat of newly signed Andy Cole from Newcastle we came really close to winning the league, losing out to Blackburn Rovers by a solitary point on the last day of the season. We were also in the final of the FA Cup.

A couple of friends from volleyball, Conrad Andrew Novack Junior or CJ (well you would do the same wouldn't you!) and Teresa Sorenson, helped me persuade the Crystal City Sports Pub to televise the game. I supplied them with United shirts for the big event. When I asked Teresa if she liked football she said it was okay and that her brother played. She called it soccer until I corrected her. She had only ever heard of one team and of course it was Manchester United.

Kick off was at 10.00am local time. It was too early for a beer so we settled for a Mimosa each. By the end of the disappointing game that we lost to a Paul Rideout goal, we were well into the draught Bass that was as close to a real beer that we could find. We decided to go back to our apartments to freshen up and then go into the city. On the way back we stopped into Fred's place, the bar in The Holiday Inn. The bar tender was a native American with the longest and straightest hair I'd ever seen on a man. When we staggered in, still dressed in our match day colours he said, "Guys, I can't believe we lost, have a drink on me." United really is a global club with global fans.

Although it was easy to keep fit while living in DC, it was not easy to find a game of football and I had to make do with the odd kick around in a park. The conditions of the field were so bad that I longed for the good old mud and puddles of Boggart Hole Clough. We did manage a game one Sunday against a group of Mexicans who hardly spoke any English, not that it mattered because football is a universal language. There were five of us, CJ, Teresa, her brother Troy who was about fifteen at the time, and a colleague who was visiting from the UK called Dylan. There were five of them. Teresa had never played before but she was an athlete who had excelled at Basketball in High School. She was also tenacious. A couple of minutes into the game, she robbed one of the opposition players, kicked it past another and then blasted the ball into the goal left footed. I believe that was when I first realized that she was the girl for me.

Another Double and The Arndale

The new season arrived with still no sign of Eric's return. Instead of the excitement welcoming some famous new players to look forward to we were all shocked when the boss sold Andrei Kanchelskis to Everton, Paul Ince to Inter Milan and Mark Hughes to Chelsea. Lee Sharpe had earlier been sold to Leeds. The only new signings in the summer were a couple of Norwegians called Ronny Johnsen, now where had I seen him before? We also signed his fellow countryman, Ole Gunnar Solskjaer.

I was back in England for a short visit when we played the first game of the season, away to Aston Villa. It was really frightening. In the team that day were a bunch of kids that most of us had never heard of. Who did Fergie think he was, Matt Busby? We were three down at half time and only managed to salvage some pride with a goal in the second half. Losing the first game of the season 3-1 could usually be stomached but not when we had no idea what the manager was doing. That night on Match of the Day some geezer called Alan Hansen said that you don't win anything with kids. Well nobody had since Busby in the halcyon days of the Babes. Hansen was supposed to be an expert pundit and we all feared the worst.

Frantically I started to read about David Beckham and the Neville brothers and Paul Scholes and Nicky Butt. They had all played alongside Ryan Giggs in the remarkable youth team that conquered all before them. The boss was seeing their development every day and he was talking them up at every interview. They recovered with a few good results and were soon in second place, beyond the runaway leaders Newcastle.

By Christmas the Geordies were twelve points clear, although we did have a game or two in hand as I recall. Eric was back and he seemed to have an effect on the younger players who were growing in confidence in every match.

At the end of 1995 I returned to the UK and immediately started playing for Great Paxton again. Fortunately they now had a reserve team and that suited my aging legs. I also invested in Sky so I could watch all the live games that United played. We were making steady progress and still had to play Newcastle at St James Park in front of their expectant and fanatical supporters. If we won, the title race was wide open again, if we lost, it was all over. In the first half, the Geordies absolutely battered us. Peter Schmeichel probably played the best half that any goalkeeper has ever played, twice denying Les Ferdinand with point blank saves. The longer the game went on, however, the more belief there seemed to be in the younger players. Mid way through the second half we started to threaten their goal, then, with about a quarter of an hour to go, it happened, Eric Cantona volleyed home the only goal of the game.

We continued to win games but so did Newcastle, although they did drop a few more points than we did, allowing us to take a slender points margin into the last couple of games. Going in to the last game of the season the Geordies still had a chance. We had to get at least a draw at Middlesborough and the title was ours. But if Newcastle won and we lost, they would be champions for the first time in half a decade. It was a time for calm, for the managers to weave their magic. Unfortunately for the Geordies, Kevin Keegan had neither magic nor calm. In a TV interview after the penultimate game he totally lost it declaring that he would; "love it, love it, love it, if we beat them." It has haunted both Keegan and the Newcastle fans ever since. For the record we slaughtered Boro on their own ground 3-0. Even Gary Pallister scored his first goal of the season. It gave us another excuse for a song that we would introduce at Wembley the following week, an adaption of Down By The Riverside that celebrated our third Premier League title in four years.

I was now dating Teresa, my blonde American friend, and she was fortunate to be visiting me in England for the season finale and the Cup final.

At Wembley the following week we faced our greatest rivals, or at least we should have done. Somebody forgot to tell Liverpool to turn up. They defended with all eleven players for most of the game, hardly getting into our half and not having one decent attempt on goal in the full ninety minutes. That said, they were somehow managing to keep us from scoring, that is until a magical Frenchman anticipated a soft headed clearance from a corner. In an instant he adjusted his body and thumped an unstoppable half volley through the whole Liverpool team into the welcoming net. It was our second double in three seasons and we were the first team to ever win the double on more than one occasion. James, Jennifer, Charlotte, Joe and I taught Teresa how to celebrate

A few weeks later, Teresa and I travelled back to the United States to finalise our wedding plans. Her parents lived in West Virginia in a town called Martinsburg. Teresa's dad, Harvey, was the Chief Ranger at Harpers Ferry Historic National Park, and we wanted to get married in the Park, on the famous Appalachian Trail (a two thousand mile hike right up the East Coast of America from the Carolinas into New England). Sandy, my future mother in law had found a Minister in Harper's Ferry who was excited at setting up the outdoor event.

Luckily, the only person we needed to get permission from to make it happen was the Chief Ranger.

On 15th June 1996, Teresa and I celebrated the completion of the arrangements at The Outback restaurant in Martinsburg. We had to wait for a table and so we did what all natural thinking people would do, we went to the bar for a drink. I will never forget what happened when we got to the bar. As I ordered a drink, a girl commented about how cute my accent was and asked where I was from. For Englishmen in America this is thankfully a regular occurrence although for the life of me I can't explain why. When I told her I was from Manchester, both her face, and the face of her boyfriend turned white. We are so sorry about the bomb they said. I had no idea what they were talking about until they nodded towards the TV above the optics on the bar. It was the day of the Arndale Centre bombing in Manchester. I will always remember where I was the day Manchester changed forever.

Hail Le Roi

Teresa and I married as planned in August 1996. James was the best man, Jenny and Charlotte were beautiful bridesmaids and Joe stole the show. Andrea and I competed for most tears when the bridesmaids walked across the grass spreading rose petals. Teresa's brother Troy was an usher and his friend Tommy gave us the keys to his father's Corvette to drive back to Martinsburg. It was probably a very stupid thing to do, especially for a newlywed, but I slammed that car as fast as it would go along the quiet country roads, topping a hundred and twenty on one of the longer stretches. Thankfully, we both arrived back at the Sorenson house safe and sound for the reception.

James, who was thirteen at the time made a great speech, telling everybody that he was a bit nervous but that was because it was the first time for him doing this kind of thing, not like his Dad. Cheeky blighter! Later that night, Teresa, James and I changed out of our glad rags into United shirts, it only seemed fitting for the double, double winners to play a part.

That close season, Alan Shearer turned down the opportunity to join United for the second time. Shearer had joined Blackburn from Southampton a couple of years earlier because they offered him a shed load of money. This time he was really close to joining us when Keegan stepped in, offering to match any terms on offer at Old Trafford. Shearer was a Geordie through and through and the chance to join his boyhood team and help them win the title for the first time in modern history was too much of a temptation. He never won another medal in his career.

Teresa and I, the kids and the rest of the family flew back from DC the next day. Most of us wearing our United shirts again. When we arrived at Heathrow we were informed of the Charity Shield score against Newcastle. It was 4-0 to the champions. Poor Alan Shearer; and he could have joined the biggest team in the world.

The following season lived up to expectations, especially in the first game when David Beckham scored from his own half in a 3-0 away win against Wimbledon. We could have and should have won the European Cup, now the Champions League, during this period but a strange ruling by UEFA on the number of non nationals allowed in each team penalized United more than most. We still reached the semi finals that season and would have won it but for wasteful finishing in the semi final against the eventual winners Borussia Dortmund. For a number of seasons it seemed that whoever beat United in the Champions League would go on to win it.

In the league we were unstoppable, despite a 5-0 drubbing at Newcastle that was Shearer's one and only bit of joy against United in his time with the Geordies. At the end of the season, a jubilant Eric Cantona lifted the Premier League Trophy for us for the fourth time in five years. He then left us all in tears when announcing his premature retirement from the game.

Cantona's legacy goes well beyond what he did on the field, although that was extraordinary enough. Eric will go down in the history of Manchester United as one of the greatest ever players. The fact that he never won the European Cup is a travesty. His early retirement from the game he loved robbed us of a unique talent and left an emptiness that is only matched by George Best's early retirement more than two decades earlier. The effect he had on the development of the new generation of players is something that every supporter of Manchester United should be eternally grateful for. Eric, for the short time he was with us was the King, or in his own language, Le Roi. Mercy beaucoup mon amie, et au revoir!

Living and Playing in The Desert

I lived in the UK again for just over two years, managing to play for Great Paxton on a Saturday, and often able to watch the mighty red devils as well. Sky television was now running football and the wonderful experience of a three o'clock Saturday kick off had become a rarity. More and more money was being pumped into the game and the likelihood of a successful underdog was becoming nothing more than a dream.

My job was taking me all over the world and the first thing I ever did when arriving in a new country was find out where and when I could watch United on the TV. Eventually I was asked to move to Tucson Arizona and the prospect of 300 days of sunshine every year was too much of a temptation to resist, especially when I knew that the job would include monthly visits to Europe and a smart guy like me would always be able to make his travel plans move through England.

Teresa and I were introduced to an amazing real estate broker called Hoot Gibson who showed us all around the city and dozens of houses. We eventually chose a family home in Oro Valley. Hoot was a hero in every sense of the word, a fighter pilot by trade who had seen tours in Korea, Vietnam and had also been the fifth commander of the Thunderbirds. The Thunderbirds are the US Air Force version of our Red Arrows. (I know that you were all thinking about Mr. Tracey and a bunch of puppets.) We moved into our new home in January 1998.

The season ended empty handed as United struggled to cope with the loss of Eric Cantona. Watching games was difficult but a friend told me about the Fox World

Sports Channel. It was too late for the 1998 season but I subscribed for the start of the next season.

Living in Arizona had its pluses, like the weather, and its minuses like a lack of football, poor beer and of course I was missing the kids, my parents and sister and all my friends. Teresa was happy as a sun worshipper and her family was now on the same continent so visiting would be easier and cheaper.

To combat some of the loneliness I did three things. Firstly I wrapped myself in my work that did include regular business trips back to the UK. Secondly I found a football (or soccer) team to play for and some of the guys from Truckmiller FC remain my friends today. If Truckmiller sounds like a strange name, its origin is even stranger. The team turned up for games with one of the players responsible for a crate of beer, usually Miller Lite. It would be stored during the game in the cold box on one of the players trucks, hence the name of Truckmiller. The third thing I did was linked to the second. Three of the players, Brad, Gary and BJ were forming a band. They needed a singer and I had been lead singer in a couple of bands in the early eighties. We were awful at first, but improved quickly. We practiced at the house of Curt Henneke, the drummer and another really good friend. One night, when we were in the middle of a practice, Curt's neighbor Ally banged on his front door demanding us to stop because she had an early start and the noise we were making was stopping her from sleeping. So the name 'Ally Can't Sleep' was born.

American Sports

Living in Tucson has one more drawback if you are a sports fan, there are no professional sports teams. The nearest teams are a hundred miles away in Phoenix who could boast the Suns basketball team, Coyotes Ice Hockey, and the Arizona Cardinal American Football team. They also had a rounder's team called the Diamondbacks but baseball is just one of those games that you either love or hate and I don't love it. Sports fans in Tucson only had one choice, the University of Arizona. The University was strong in a number of sports including men's Basketball and American Football.

For those who don't know, every American sport is designed around TV Commercials. They have time outs for this and time outs for that and time outs for the referees and time outs to wipe sweat off the floor. It's all a con. Time outs are there for one reason only, to stop the game to allow TV commercials. The last two minutes of a basketball game can last for an hour with a time out called every few seconds. To say it is boring is an understatement like saying that Mount Everest is a hill.

The only game I partially enjoyed was watching the Arizona Basketball team. They were always competitive and Hoot Gibson took me along to a few games. Remember that I'm old fashioned and like to stand at my sports events. Memories of United Road and the Stretford End are indelibly painted on my heart. As Keano famously said, the Old Trafford crowd today is a bunch of old corporate folk eating prawn sandwiches. Let me tell you that there is no comparison to the American sports fans. Sleeping through a game is easy.

The first summer I lived in Tucson was the year of the World Cup in France. Weekend games were easy enough to see but midweek games always happened when I was supposed to be at work. Another really good friend, Jim Rayburn was also a keen football supporter, having once played for a USA representative team in Germany. Jim was from California and a Manchester United fan. We really are everywhere. The quarter finals arrived and England were pitted against an old enemy, Argentina. Jim and I headed to the Rita Road Market that also had a café attached with a huge but grainy TV. England were playing well and David Beckham was having a particularly good game, keeping the Argentinian midfield under control while pulling the strings for England. We were one goal up before a slack bit of defending allowed an Argentina forward to equalize. Then for no apparent reason, Becks flicked a foot towards an opponent and the referee sent him off. In the last minute, Sol Campbell scored a great header and we should have gone through. Unfortunately, the referee spotted a foul that nobody else in the stadium, nor any of the millions watching on TV, saw. After extra time, England lost a tense penalty shootout and was on the plane back home. Never mind, there was always baseball on the TV through the summer.

Later that summer, Andrea chaperoned the kids for their first visit. Towards the end of their holiday, James and I managed to find United's first game of the season, live on Fox Sports World. It meant that we would be late for a party at a friend's house but I'm sure they understood. After an hour it looked bleak. Leicester City was two goals up against us at Old Trafford. We rallied and saved a point with Beckham redeeming himself with a great free kick to equalize. Free kicks were soon to become his trademark.

We needed firepower and Fergie reacted by buying Dwight Yorke from Aston Villa to complement Andy Cole, who was now called Andrew, Ole Gunnar Solskjaer and Teddy Sheringham who had slotted well into Eric Cantona's old role of deep lying striker.

Travelling the World

I will detour from a chronological history to share a few momentous occasions I've experienced watching United in the four corners of the world.

I've seen United play on TV in pubs in Chicago, Los Angeles, San Diego, Las Vegas and Washington DC amongst others in the USA and in every pub the bar has been packed with United supporters. Many were expatriates living abroad but many were Americans. I also watched us beat Wigan in the League Cup Final in a bar in Orlando in Florida.

I've watched United play in an Irish pub in Prague and another Irish pub in Stockholm. In Warsaw, a friend owns a bar called the Blue Cactus, a cross between a Mexican restaurant and Irish pub, and I've seen United play there too. In each of these cities I've been able to share a pint with fellow reds.

On one occasion I was starting a business trip to the Far East with a short layover in Honolulu. It's a rough life but somebody has to do it. On Waikiki beach there is a great restaurant and pub called Dukes. I was sitting in the bar when the bar tender gave me a drink and pointed to a guy across the bar. I was wearing a United Tee Shirt and the fellow United fan had spotted it. He was also from Manchester and mad about United. Later that trip I watched us beat Liverpool in Hooters at Clarke Quay in Singapore before travelling on to Bangkok. I had carefully planned the trip so that I would have meetings on the Friday and Monday, meaning I couldn't move on to Seoul in South Korea until the following Tuesday. I thought a weekend in Bangkok would be fun.

Unbeknown to me, the weekend I was there coincided with national elections. During the election everybody was encouraged to vote but they had to vote in the area they were registered. To ensure that all the bar and restaurant staff travelled home, the government ordered everywhere to shut down. I was in Bangkok with nowhere to go. Our country manager and my host, Joe, was certain he could find somewhere that was open and we headed out of the Marriott on Sukhamvit Road towards the nearby Cowboy Plaza. If you've never been to Bangkok you are probably imagining a neat shopping centre or trendy area with bars and restaurants. Not this plaza. Cowboy plaza ran underneath the overhead monorail and was a long row of shacks with tin roofs and rollover doors. As we approached, a couple of local girls jumped up from a bench and asked if we wanted a beer. You have probably guessed the answer and they told us to go to the ninth door on the left, a red one, knock three times and they would let us in. The girls seemed nice enough and so we headed in the direction of the door, found it and were duly allowed into a small candlelit room with a pool table, a small bar with draught beer – now that was a luxury – and about ten patrons, all English. We ordered a beer, had a friendly chat with the girls who ran the place and the other Brits and then the phone rang. Immediately one of the girls put her finger to her mouth, telling us to be silent, and another blew out the candles. Through the crack in the door we could see blue and red flashing lights and could hear the slow rolling of car tyres. It was the longest thirty seconds of my life and I was rehearsing the explanations when I would finally be released from a Bangkok prison. Luckily, the car kept rolling on and as soon as we got the all clear we graciously thanked the girls for the drinks and got the hell out of there.

The next time I visited Bangkok was a little less sensational. I did, however, give up the opportunity of a Thai massage because United were playing Bolton and it was televised in the bar where I met Joe. Ole Solskjaer scored a last minute equalizer before I rejoined the guys in a bar with a live band from the Philippines. I should have realized as soon as I walked in that I had been set up. I was immediately showed to the stage where I belted out Free's 'All Right Now', the Commitments version of 'Mustang Sally' and Steppenwolf's 'Born to be Wild' before enjoying free beer for the rest of the night.

My only other visit to Bangkok included a trip to the Lumpinee Stadium, home of Thai Boxing. Now that was a crazy crowd. Most people seemed to spend more time betting on their favorite boxer, rather than actually watching the fights. It reminded me of the hooligan crowds of the late seventies and early eighties. The boxing itself was great fun.

I've also had the pleasure of watching United on televisions in Seoul, Taiwan, Manila, Abu Dhabi and Dubai in the Emirates, Cairo, Jordan and Riyadh. More of that later!

Thank God for Satellite and T'Internet

A lot of people complain about Sky television ruining football. My friend Tony in Great Paxton still refuses to buy it. I myself share a lot of disappointment that football is no longer a game for working people and that it has lost its' identity. It is also a shame that Saturday at 3pm is nowhere near as magical a time as it used to be. We are now drowned in televised football.

However, on a purely selfish note, I would never have been able to see the mighty red devils across the world without Sky and the other Satellite companies and for that reason alone I am so grateful.

The other revolution in technology is the internet, or T'internet as Bolton comedian Peter Kay loves to call it. The internet has kept me up to date with transfer gossip, with injury news and other important aspects of the greatest sport on the planet and the greatest team in the world. I log in to the official Manchester United website at least three times a week. I also log in to the BBC and Sky Sports sites and occasionally write on the Red Café blog and forum under the pseudonym of Tucson Manc (original eh!)

So while in many respects life is more complicated and a lot less personal than it used to be, I say let's play the hand that we are dealt and get on with it.

Scaring the Neighbours

The 1998/99 season was going to be make or break for United. Arsenal had just won the league title again and looked like a very good team. In true United style we bounced back even stronger and as we all know that season is the greatest in our history and the history of any other football club or sports franchise.

United were playing scintillating football with the best midfield in the world chosen from any four from Beckham, Butt, Giggs, Keane, Scholes and Swedish winger Jesper Blomqvist. In defence the pairing of big Jaap Stam and Ronny Johnsen was as good as the previous Bruce/Pallister one. Gary Neville was a terrific right full back and Dennis Irwin was a marvel at left back. Up front, we had four of the best strikers in the world vying for two positions. It didn't matter who Alex Ferguson played, the team could and usually did beat all before them.

Our great rivals again that year were Arsenal and the league would go down to the last weekend. Before that, we had the simple matter of the Champions League and FA Cup to deal with. In Europe we had knocked out perennial favorites AC Milan and were facing Juventus in the semi final. In the FA Cup we were drawn against Arsenal. Massive games were coming thick and fast. The first leg of the European Cup was played at Old Trafford and I watched the game in my living room in Tucson. United had all the possession but didn't create many chances. On a breakaway, Juventus scored and it looked ominous until Sheringham released Giggs with a typically clever pass and the Welsh winger fired home the equalizer. The FA Cup semi final was played ten days later and despite dominating a ten man Arsenal team, the game ended as a 1-1 draw. We now had an FA Cup semi final replay and a Champions League semi final to play with a key league game sandwiched in-between. The most upsetting thing though was that I was heading over to Saudi Arabia and unsure if I would even get the chance to watch the games.

After thirty hours of travelling, I eventually got to the Hyatt in Riyadh at about midnight. I was unsure of the time in England but switched on the TV in the room and flicked through the channels. A couple of Arab football pundits that I recognized were talking and I hoped to pick up the score. As I started to wearily unpack the highlights came on. First a Beckham goal, then an Arsenal equalizer. Next was the final straw, or so I thought, Roy Keane had been dismissed. A few moments later, Phil Neville who was playing at left back clumsily tackled the Arsenal winger and the referee pointed to the spot. The clock said it was already ninety minutes into the game and I was sure that we were out. Enter the great Dane. Peter Schmeichel had been one of the best goalkeepers in history and had already announced he would be leaving us at the end of the season. The penalty was taken and Peter dived full length to his left, making a miraculous save. I couldn't believe it, especially when I found out that I had arrived in time to see extra time. Could we do it with ten men? I should have known better and Ryan Giggs scored one of the best individual goals of all time to take us into the final. I was a mess at the meeting the following day because I had only managed about an hour of sleep, but I obviously didn't worry too much and allowed adrenalin to get me through the day.

Flights out of Saudi Arabia for the UK usually leave around 2.00am, allowing a breakfast arrival in London.

On the last day of the trip, United faced Juventus in the second leg of the Champions League. I had a dinner meeting that evening and raced back to the hotel to catch whatever I could of the game. I arrived with about twenty minutes gone and couldn't believe my eyes, Juventus were beating us 2-0. Roy Keane inspired United to one of the greatest ever comebacks in a game that ranks amongst the best he ever played, especially considering that he was booked and if United could overcome the Italians, he would miss the final. United did come back and won 3-2 in sensational style with a last minute winner. I made the flight with less than five minutes to spare.

We were now in two finals and had a great chance of winning the league. All we had to do was beat Tottenham at Old Trafford on the last day of the season.

The Sunday after flying back from Saudi was greeted with tremendous anticipation. Teresa had by now accepted that when United played an important game she would either watch it somewhere else, or just stay out of the way. She couldn't bear to watch all the emotions I went through, and some of the language put her off a bit as well. On this occasion she tended to the garden.

She was chatting to the next door neighbours when David Beckham equalised , and had to explain that my shouting and screaming was normal when United played. When Andy Cole put us in the lead and I screamed again, even louder, they both came in to see what had happened. "You're scaring the neighbours, she said." As if I cared, we had just won the league again.

The Treble and Almost Kicking The Bucket

The next stop was Wembley and an FA Cup Final against Newcastle. Was this going to be a great double or was Alan Shearer going to actually win a medal with Newcastle?

I was gutted to find that the game was not televised in Tucson. I don't know if it was a dispute, or it was on a pay per view channel that I couldn't find but I had to listen on an internet streamed radio station. Scholes and Sheringham scored in a 2-0 victory that flattered a poor Newcastle performance. Two trophies down and two trophies won. Could we make it a treble against Bayern Munich in the final in Barcelona.

We had played Munich twice in the group stage of that seasons Champions League. We had twice dominated them, only to be pegged back for 1-1 and 2-2 draws. The final would ordinarily have held no fears for United, but without the talismanic Roy Keane and the rapidly improving Paul Scholes who was also suspended, United were up against it. Perhaps there was an omen in our favour, the final was being played on what would have been Sir Matt Busby's ninetieth birthday. Could fate provide a helping hand?

Jim Rayburn took the day off and joined me for the big game. Dave Taft also said he would come around on the day he was leaving the company. We were also joining Dave later that evening at his leaving dinner at L'il Abners Steak House.

Jim came around at eleven o'clock, forty five minutes before the kick off. The fridge was stocked with

Boddingtons Draught-flow and Samuel Adams, the best beers I could find. Jim brought the ingredients for his special Bloody Mary's. We had no horseradish so I suggested using English mustard instead. Jim was reluctant so I gave him a jar and told him to try it. Has he dug the tea spoon in I knew what was coming next. "That's not bad," he said before his expression changed and sweat started to pour. When he recovered he made the best Bloody Mary I've ever had. By kick off we were drinking the beer and settled down to watch what we hoped would be a historic game. As usual, the boys in red didn't let us down.

The game started badly and we were 1-0 down within five minutes. Half time arrived and we hadn't really created anything in front of the German goal. The second half wasn't much better and but for a couple of typically brilliant Peter Schmeichel saves and the woodwork twice, we would have been further behind. With the game ticking away into injury time it began to look unlikely that Alex Ferguson would repeat the glory of his illustrious predecessor. But this is Manchester United we are talking about. I looked at Jim and suggested that a double was a fairly good season and that we would be back again next year. I was heading towards the fridge for my umpteenth can when we forced a corner on the left. There was a quick scramble in the box, Giggs struck a shot that found its way to Teddy Sheringham who swiveled to guide the ball into the net. 1-1 and we had done it, the Germans looked demoralized and we would surely take them in extra time. I jumped in the air and started to scream. "Yeeeesss!" I cried over and over again. Still jumping until suddenly I saw stars, went dizzy and fell down. When I came to I looked towards the TV and saw David Beckham taking a corner in what I thought was a repeat of the equalizing goal. Teddy rose at the near post to head the ball – wait a minute I was sure he had scored with his right foot – Teddy flicked the ball towards the goal and Ole Solskjaer stretched out a leg to fire us ahead. 2-1 to United. I looked at Jim and smiled, still unable to get off my knees. United were champions of Europe again and I started to sob like a baby.

In typical US style, Dave Taft arrived just in time to watch us lift the trophy before helping himself to whatever was left in the fridge. When the game was over and I had sufficiently recovered we made fish and chips before singing 'We Are The Champions' over and over, interwoven with the occasional 'Champions of Europe'. The phone rang and James Jennifer and Charlotte each took turns to tell me we were Champions of Europe again. They had watched the game in Great Paxton. That night at L'il Abners, and thankfully Teresa drove us there because we were talking in riddles by now, Jim and I were still in our United shirts, Dave swapped his cowboy hat for a United cap and the three of us disrupted the festivities with several renditions of the United songs I had taught them.

Later that week I played for Truckmiller when Don Tocci asked how I felt and wasn't I a little sad for Lother Matteus. The German player had made his farewell to football after receiving his runners up medal in Barcelona. What kind of a silly bloody question was that? No Don, I did not feel sorry for the vanquished and defeated captain of our Champions League opponents. I only felt delirious joy that we were once again the Champions of Europe. Is it any wonder that baseball is the national sport in America? That said, Don is a good lad and he often watched live games at my house in Tucson.

The Commonwealth Games

Following the treble season was never going to be easy and United had to settle for just the league title. An accomplishment we achieved again the following year making it three in a row. Sir Alex Ferguson as he now was following a visit to Her Majesty shortly after the treble, had achieved another treble that nobody had ever done before, three titles on the bounce.

In 2001, Teresa gave birth to my fifth child, a beautiful daughter called Alexis, though she quickly became known as Lexi.

Shortly after her birth, the world changed forever. The date was September 11th 2001. I was in a hotel in El Segundo, Los Angeles when I saw the events at the New York World Trade Centre unfold on TV.

It was a very disappointing 2002 season that saw us trophy less for the first time in many a year with Arsenal making matters worse by claiming their second double.

The only real accomplishment for Manchester in 2002 was the hosting of the Commonwealth Games. Sadly the American TV networks didn't even know that the Games were on, after all it was baseball season, and my following was mainly by the internet. Manchester had to be rebuilt after the bomb attacks in 1996 and the city, like a phoenix, rose from the ashes and became one of the finest in the world. I am not being biased here but I've travelled to all the great cities in the world and Manchester is right up there.

The docks in Salford became Salford Quays with promenades and shopping centres and restaurants and bars and views towards Old Trafford. I remember when the docks were starting to get run down and there were more rats there than people. The Quays are fantastic and living there is amongst the most desirable places to live in the country. It is also the home of the North West water sports centre where many of our World champion rowers train. Castlefield at the end of Deansgate was also rebuilt, as was the Arndale Centre, this time with style rather than the old toilet block design of the original. Sports arenas were built to accommodate the games and the velodrome for cycling events and Olympic standard swimming pool are magnificent. The greatest stadium in the world also got some competition. To facilitate the athletics at the games the city built a stadium at Eastlands, holding almost fifty thousand people. Once the games were over, the City of Manchester Stadium became the home of Manchester City Football Club, enabling them to leave the run down Maine Road.

Linking everything together was a state of the art new Metro system. In addition, old theatres were refurbished and new theatres built, including the absolutely fantastic Lowry Theatre and Art Gallery at Salford Quays.

A Tottenham fan colleague complemented 'us Mancs' on a fantastic Commonwealth Games that were a tremendous advert for Britain. The problem, he said, was that London would now get the Olympics and make a right cock of it. This prophecy came from an East Ender and the first part is now true, let's hope our cockney friends don't make the second part come true and we do in fact have a great Olympics in 2012. Unfortunately, having a London centric Olympics is asking for trouble. There are so many precedents of disastrous failures, including the debacle around the redevelopment of Wembley Stadium. That project cost around double the original estimates and its completion was severely delayed.

Los Angeles

Fergies reaction to losing the title was to invest heavily on bringing Rio Ferdinand from Leeds. The previous season we had leaked a few goals and Fergie brought in the stylish defender to reverse the trend. It worked because United were once again crowned League Champions in 2003.

I was starting to get homesick by now. Life in Tucson was fun and I was playing more football than I had since I was a teenager. I was also still enjoying singing for Ally Can't Sleep and a band that spawned from Ally with the strange name of Stacked Revolver. We mixed classic rock with contemporary tunes and also added a few originals for good measure. I was actually earning a semi decent second income as well. There is a song by American band 'Canned Heat' called 'Going up the Country' that contains the line – "We might even, leave the USA" and I always added "And go back to Manchester."

Instead of me returning to Manchester, Manchester came to me. At the end of the 2003 season, United toured America. The tour took in New York, Philadelphia, Seattle and Los Angeles. All games except Los Angeles sold out in a matter of hours, faster than local American football teams would sell their tickets. I went to the Los Angeles game against a Mexican side. Before applying for tickets I rustled around a few mates to establish interest. I ended up applying for eight tickets and was successful. Then a strange thing happened. United sold the most recognizable footballer on the planet, David Beckham, to Real Madrid. Half the so called friends I'd got tickets for suddenly didn't want to go. One of them didn't even think he should pay me until I explained that it might be bad for his health. I also made sure he didn't play in the same team as me ever again when I shamed him in front of our teammates.

The event in LA was great because it was the first time in several years that I was able to watch United play in the flesh. United won the game 3-1, rounding off a successful four game win streak. Then we headed back to our hotel in Redondo Beach. The journey back was a strange one. The game had been played at the Los Angeles Coliseum, home of the 1984 Olympic Games and it is located in one of the most undesirable areas I've ever seen. I certainly wouldn't recommend a visit to a friend. It was several miles of hiking later that we finally managed to find a taxi that was willing to stop to pick us up.

Ronnie's Debut

A number of things happened that summer that changed the face of football. I've already mentioned that we sold Beckham to Real, but that didn't matter because Ole Gunnar Solskjaer was just as good and ready to take his place on the right side of midfield. Unfortunately he was injured on the first game of the new season. A few weeks later in a Champions League game he aggravated the injury and never really recovered. A Russian called Roman Abramovich also bought Chelsea. At the time, transfer fees had started to stabilize, but Abramovich changed all that. He spent hundreds of millions of pounds on players, turning Chelsea from a good team to genuine title contenders. With an eye on the future, Sir Alex bought a seventeen year old Portugese winger from Sporting Lisbon. His name was Cristiano Ronaldo.

2003 was the year that my Dad celebrated his seventieth birthday in August and Teresa, Lexi and I came over for the festivities. Teresa's Mum and Dad, Sandy and Harvey Sorenson, also visited England for the first time ever.

Having seen my beloved Manchester United again in Los Angeles, I pulled out all the stops to get a couple of tickets for the season opener against Bolton at Old Trafford. The seats were to the left of the goal at the Scoreboard End, now strangely called the East Stand, where is the imagination? They were also in front of the disabled section, providing a really crappy worm eye view. Harvey had seen just about every kind of professional American sport but never anything like this. He was amazed at the plasma TV's under the stand, the spick and span toilets and of course, the noise. Sixty eight thousand starved fans ready to cheer on the champions. Ole Gunnar looked sharp on the right side of midfield, Keano marshaled the troops and Ruud Van Nistelroy looked menacing up front. In a cagey first half where the boys attacked the East Stand (I still can't get over that) all we had to shout for was a majestic Ryan Giggs free kick, 1-0 to the champions at the interval.

The second half was much better with wave after wave of reds attacking the West Stand (If the East Stand is a bad enough name, replacing the legendary Stretford End with a West Stand is a real joke). Three goals and a missed penalty and the final score was 4-0. Ole had limped off in the second half and little did we know at the time that his appearances would be limited until the injury finally forced his retirement three years later. His replacement was the young winger I mentioned earlier. What happened next was so good it was scary. Ronaldo ran and dribbled, and crossed and absolutely terrorized the Bolton defence. His stepovers had defenders falling over themselves and he set up the fourth goal. By the end of the game the fans were shouting – "There's only one Ronaldo," which was remarkable considering there was a more famous Brazilian with the same name.

Every time I speak to Harvey since that game he asks how the young Portugese lad is doing.

The early promise led to disappointment and Arsenal regained the league title. We did, however, get to the FA Cup Final.

Ye Olde Jolly Carter's and Millwall

Our opponents at Wembley were Millwall. The kick off time in Tucson was seven in the morning.

During the bank holiday weekend at the beginning of May (it's called Memorial Day in the States), I had built a bar in the back garden. The design of the bar was tiki, which is Hawaiian, made of bamboo and usually with a sand floor. Although the bar was tiki, its' name was definitely English. Ye Olde Jolly Carter's was to be officially opened at the Cup Final.

Brad and Don from Truckmiller came, as did Jim Rayburn and a great couple called Rick and Kathy who had lived in Munich. Teresa was on fish and chip duty but for the kick off we had bacon butties. Jim made his famous Bloody Mary's and we all settled down to watch the game.

The predicted one sided final materialized and United ran out 3-0 winners with a masterful display from Ronaldo, scoring one goal, matched by the predatory Ruud scoring the other two.

After the game came the official opening of the Jolly's ,as Lexi soon started to call it. Brad suggested I open a tip jar and he put the first dollar into a red plastic cup. That dollar, and a few more, are still in the Jolly's to this day. The party went on all day until we poured the last of the guests into a taxi after dark. The following day, saw Truckmiller a couple of players short as we nursed our hangovers.

In the summer, United held off a cheeky bid from Newcastle for the Everton starlet Wayne Rooney and we looked forward to a new season with the best two teenagers in the world lining up for United, Rooney and Ronaldo.

The new team was starting to take shape but we were a bit behind Chelsea whose patriarch, Abramovich, was buying just about every world class player he could get his hands on. Chelsea's quarter billion pound investment soon paid off and they won the title in 2005 and 2006, although our progress was evident in 2006 as we ran them all the way, just failing by a couple of points.

One of the darker points in our history was happening off the field. The Manchester United Supporters Trust had managed to fight and win against Rupert Murdoch's takeover, gaining support from the Monopolies Commission amongst others because of the Sky companies growing influence on our game. They were powerless though in taking on a calculated takeover by American tycoon Malcolm Glazer. The acrimonious takeover between 2003 and 2005 has been covered by many writers, supporters and others and I won't labour the point here. Living in America, I was teased and tormented by everybody I knew that our beloved team now belonged to them. It soon became a joke too far and led to many arguments. I don't like that our beloved club is owned by foreigners any more than the next fan, and I'm convinced that the club is no longer in touch with the fans. But it won't stop me attending games; if I can afford the tickets. The trouble with United is that they are so popular, and remain so successful, that the stadium is still full for every home game. The paradox for real fans, especially those who can't afford to go to games any more, is do we want success, that keeps the stadium full, or do we want to join the ranks of the wannabe's. Either way, the ticket prices won't come down.

In the League Cup (I've lost count of its constant name changes) we played Wigan in the 2005 final, slaughtering them 4-0. In 2006, we reached the FA Cup final and totally outplayed Arsenal in a similar fashion to how we beat Liverpool a decade earlier. This time we had no Eric Cantona and couldn't find the goal. Although Rio did put the ball in the net in the second half, the linesman flagged for something, whether it was offside, which would have been a mistake, or a foul, that nobody else saw, we may never know. Once again we had been robbed of a trophy as Arsenal beat us in a penalty shoot-out.

I managed to get to Old Trafford again the following season for the third round FA Cup game against Aston Villa. James and I had a couple of beers in The Trafford before the game, then a shed full in the Bishop's Blaize immediately after. If only the singing at the game was as loud and passionate as it is in those two pubs.

The other highlight was of course the thrashing of AC Roma at Old Trafford in the quarter finals of the Champions League. Jim Rayburn and I watched the game one lunchtime at Risky Business Sports Bar on Craycroft Road in Tucson. Even after all these years it is one of the best team performances I've ever seen. I wish I could have been at Old Trafford to see it live.

The reds, with Cristiano Ronaldo and Wayne Rooney now established as world stars, the peerless Paul Scholes and Ryan Giggs still pulling the strings, and another rock of a defensive partnership in Ferdinand and Nemanja Vidic, supported well by the flying Patrice Evra at left back and ever willing captain Gary Neville on the right, were ready for a real challenge at the title. All the money in the world couldn't stop us and we won the league again with three games to spare. United were back in their rightful place as champions of England after three barren years. We could have been celebrating a glorious double but lost a poor FA Cup final to Chelsea. Another perfectly good goal, this time by Giggs, was disallowed and a Drogba winner in extra time sealed our fate.

In the summer we were back in England to celebrate my parents Golden Wedding. Jim and Eileen Carter had been married six months before the Munich Air Disaster and their love was as strong as ever fifty years later. I had been trying to get back to England for a couple of years but this time it looked more promising, I was headhunted by a recruitment company and joined an outsourcing company in November.

Return of The Prodigal

The global credit crunch had started and we were unable to sell our house in Tucson so Teresa and I were once again living in separate countries. I was now living in Salford Quays and commuting to Prescott near Liverpool every day. Working near Liverpool was strange for a lifetime United fan but I did have a few allies, including Pete Gillon who I often meet for a pre-game beer.

I had always kept my membership to United throughout the ten years I'd been in the States and now I was able to put it to use, watching the champions on many occasions as they defended their title. It may be that I'm older now, but the atmosphere at our home games is not the same. It's almost as if the crowd is saying that we've paid all this money to come here, now you must entertain us. Maybe the theatre of dreams is now the home to theatre lovers who only clap at the end of an act or at the final curtain. There are exceptions and two of these happened in the 2008 season.

I had a ticket for the Stretford End in the FA cup against Arsenal. We won 4-0 and the Stretford End was rocking. We even stood for long periods in the game. The second was against Barcelona in the semi final of the Champions League.

I was living in an apartment block adjacent to the Lowry shopping centre and across the square from the magnificent Lowry theatre. My flat overlooks the Manchester Ship Canal, and just beyond that is the Theatre of Dreams. I sleep with the curtains open and the last thing at night and first thing in the morning that I see is the red neon sign that reads 'Manchester United'. The car park has some astonishing cars and one of the Penthouse slots had two Bentley's. I arrived at the same time as one of the Bentley's on one occasion and held open the door for an athletic looking guy in a grey hoodie. He ignored me and when I said Hi he again ignored me by looking down at the floor in the lift. It was a few days later when I watched a game on the television that I recognized that I had shared the lift with Nicolas Anelka and there were strong rumours that Fergie might try to buy him. Thankfully he went to Chelsea. The difference in class between the guy in the lift at Imperial Point and the two in the lift at the Ritz Carlton a dozen years earlier was immense.

Shortly after I arrived back in England, Jennifer, who lives in Tucson, announced that she was pregnant and my beautiful grand-daughter Amelia was born in June. If she had told me that she was expecting before I left, I may still be living in Tucson, but life is like that.

Although I had been successful in applying for tickets around mid-season, as the likelihood of glory grew, the chances of being selected in the ticket ballot was becoming remote. I firmly believe that Old Trafford would regularly sell out if it held a hundred thousand, rather than the seventy six thousand of today's capacity. I tried and failed to get tickets for the last three home games in the league, and for the home quarter final against Roma and home semi final against Barcelona in the Champions League. As I contemplated my bad luck and the unfairness of the prawn sandwich society that Old Trafford has become, my mobile phone rang. One of my allies at work, Pete Collins, asked if I wanted to join him in an Executive Box for the semi against Barcelona. Apparently, his father in law had booked a box through his company to host a couple of clients from Barcelona. Unluckily for them, but lucky for me, the Spanish company was having trouble and the businessmen had to stay in Spain to take care of business. I was going to the game.

The Executive Boxes at Old Trafford are luxurious and the food is surprisingly good. The three course meal included rack of lamb, which is one of my favourites, and the beer and wine flowed way beyond what a normal liver can cope with. The box had ten seats. Our host was actually a Manchester City fan but he used the box at Old Trafford for business entertainment. Pete's father in law and his two brothers were all Leeds fans and shock of all shocks, one of the brothers had brought his son and he was a Liverpool fan. Fortunately another United fan joined us, making it three with Pete and myself. Watching a game live at Old Trafford, behind a sheet of glass with some Leeds and Liverpool fans was surreal, but at least I was there. The box in question was behind the goal at the scoreboard end, giving us a great view down the pitch. When the game started all alcohol had to be removed from the room, not that we needed any more.

The first leg had ended without a goal and so it was all to play for. All of our big players were there and Barcelona had the little genius Lionel Messi in their side. Messi is one of the best players I've ever seen and every time he received the ball it spelled danger. The game as you can imagine was cagey because there was so much to play for. A Paul Scholes wonder goal into the net below us was the only score of the game and we were going to Moscow to take on Chelsea in the final. I don't think anybody sat down during the game and the stadium was bouncing to the sounds of seventy thousand singing reds. I skipped the whole way back to

Imperial Point, after a couple of celebratory beers in the lounge near the Executive Box.

Champions of Europe – Again

Being relatively new to the area, at least this time around, I was unsure where to watch the final and I eventually chose the Lime Bar at the Lowry centre. I had been there for a pre-game pint on a couple of occasions and expected a big and boisterous crowd. By contrast, it was surprisingly quiet but there were a few fellow reds and a solitary Chelsea fan, shame on him. I'm not going to spend too much time here detailing the game because that has already been done by countless others. I remember hugging and kissing complete strangers when Ronaldo put us ahead with a brilliant header, then lamenting the missed chances that should have seen us three nil up before half time. The ricochet that found itself at Frank Lampards' unmarked feet just before half time added to the tension in the Lime Bar and no doubt in thousands of other bars across the world. It remained one goal each until the final whistle and then again through extra time. We could barely watch and were in shock when Ronaldo had his penalty saved. Could Edwin Van Der Sar, our best keeper since the great Peter Schmeichel, keep us in the game. The screams of delight and relief when John Terry missed the final kick that would have relegated us to runners up were probably heard at my parents house five miles away. It was nip and tuck until my favourite ex neighbour, Nicolas Anelka, walked nervously up to the penalty area. Van Der Sar did it, saving brilliantly to his right and we were champions of Europe again. I've never seen any of the people that I shared that amazing evening with again, I'm not even sure that I would recognize them; but for a couple of hours, they were my best friends in the world. The mobile rang shortly after the final whistle as Lexi and Teresa celebrated with me from the other side of the Atlantic.

Fifty years after the Munich Air Disaster and Manchester United provided the most fitting tribute imaginable; they became the Champions of Europe for the third time.

Shortly afterwards, Manchester City were purchased by a consortium from the United Arab Emirates. It has been 33 years since City won their last trophy but that may all change now. The new owners are threatening to make the spending of Roman Abramovich at Chelsea seem trivial. My brother in law, Phil, is a true blue and excited by the prospect of challenging for trophies again on a regular basis. We will all have to wait and see what happens next at Eastlands.

Later that summer, James married his long time girlfriend Nikki and for the first time in a long time, we were all together, including Teresa, Jennifer, Lexi and Amelia from Tucson. Teresa and Lexi would stay for five months. James, like his father before him, wore a Manchester United shirt on his wedding day. It was under his Royal Marine uniform but we all knew he was wearing it.

The Future is Bright

The red flag is certainly flying high again and the team is young and still improving. We are not sure how many more seasons we will get from Sir Alex and his successor will have massive shoes to fill. Sir Alex Ferguson is the most successful manager in history and we are fortunate to have had both he and Sir Matt Busby shaping the history of our magnificent club.

As I finish this potted history of my life to date with Manchester United, we are approximately half way through the 2008/2009 season, and United are well placed. We have also just become the World Club Champions, having successfully represented Europe in Japan in December.

Teresa and Lexi have just left Salford after five months of visiting and touring the country. Lexi, who is the fifth sibling to follow their father as a United fan, managed to get to two games; the home tie against Bolton in the league that we won 2-0 and the 5-3 drubbing of Blackburn in the League Cup that is now sponsored by Carling. We shall all be back together again soon, perhaps in Tucson, hopefully in Salford.

I feel sorry for the kids today. They may have a thousand channels to choose from on the TV. They have their iPods and their Nintendo Wii's and Xboxes. They have their mobile phones and countless other gadgets that we would never have dreamed of. But they don't have the Stretford End or United Road and ticket prices are so high that they can hardly afford to go to the games. Part of the joy for me was queuing up outside the turnstile in anticipation of the game. These kids don't have that. The camaraderie that comes with standing in the same place, with familiar faces all around you for each and every home game has gone. We are where we are and we cannot halt progress but not everything changes for the better.

As I write these final few words I glance over my shoulder towards Old Trafford. The sun is shining but it is a bitterly cold winter's day. Sky Sports News is on in the background and many games have been cancelled up and down the country. Old Trafford looks majestic, rising above all the nearby architecture through a light mist.

Let's hope that the future continues to shine on the wonderful game of football and our beloved Manchester United. And, perhaps we can all long for a return to terracing. All it should take is for the powers that be to get their collective heads together and look at the facts; instead of making knee jerk reactions like the one that led to all seater stadiums. It is the only way that we can hope to return the game to the people it really belongs to, the fans; ordinary working class people like you and me.

In my life I've seen the Trinity of Best, Law and Charlton, I've seen Bryan Robson, Ryan Giggs and Roy Keane, I have seen Eric Cantona and Paul Scholes and now I look forward to seeing the further development of Wayne Rooney and Cristiano Ronaldo. Boy have I been lucky.

Keep the red flag flying. I did, all the way from Salford to Tucson and back again.

Printed in the United Kingdom by
Lightning Source UK Ltd., Milton Keynes
141556UK00001B/333/P